What people are saying about
Modern Media Relations for Nonprofits

"After 20 years in journalism, the biggest weakness I've witnessed in nonprofits is a lack of staff trained to handle the media. So often, I experience small mistakes that make a huge difference in an organization's ability to make their message heard. *Modern Media Relations for Nonprofits* is a concise, approachable resource for nonprofits to get the best exposure possible—earned media—without increasing their budget, or even staffing, if resources are allocated correctly."

—Stephanie Carson
Producer NC Public News Service
and editorial director, Women AdvaNCe

"*Modern Media Relations for Nonprofits* is an essential guide for today's nonprofit professional. Whether you're promoting a feel-good story or tackling a public-relations crisis, you'll find the help you need quickly and clearly."

—Claire Meyerhoff
President of The Planned Giving Agency, LLC
and former Washington-based broadcast journalist
for CNN, CBS Radio and Sirius XM

"Today's media environment isn't just fast-paced—it's instantaneous. Working successfully with the media requires nonprofits to combine new approaches, like reaching out to reporters on Twitter, with old standbys like telling a really good story. This book is the perfect guide to making old and new work together effectively."

—Kivi Leroux Miller
Founder and CEO of Nonprofit Marketing Guide

Modern Media Relations for Nonprofits:

Modern Media
Relations
for Nonprofits:

Creating an Effective PR Strategy for Today's World

By Peter Panepento & Antionette G. Kerr
Foreword by Kivi Leroux Miller

BOLD & BRIGHT
MEDIA

Published by Bold & Bright Media, LLC.
319 Becks Church Road
Lexington, North Carolina 27292
Boldandbrightmedia.com

ISBN-13: 978-0692830734
ISBN-10: 0692830731

Library of Congress Control Number: 2017961149

Bold & Bright Media is a multimedia publishing company committed to bold hearts, bright minds, and storytellers whose experiences will inspire and compel others to grow in their own greatness. For more information visit BoldandBrightMedia.com.

Dedications

To my three children, each of whom provides wonderful inspiration every day. —*Peter Panepento*

To the legacy of former UNC-Chapel Hill professor and advisor, Charles Sumner "Chuck" Stone, Jr.; a veteran journalist, NABJ co-founder, media revolutionary and ombudsman to the soul! —*Antionette Kerr*

We both wish to extend thanks to our families, and strategy gurus and friends Kivi Leroux Miller, James Loy, Jr., The Sisterhood, Attorney Robert Monath, Stephanie Carson, Denise Brosseau and Claire Meyerhoff.

Contents

Part 2: G. is Goal Oriented

Part 3: R. is Responsive

Part 6: T. is Targeted

Foreword
By Kivi Leroux Miller

Where do you get your news?

If I asked this question 20 years ago, your answer might include the daily paper that appeared at your doorstep, drive-time radio, and the 6 p.m. or 11 p.m. television newscasts.

Today, your response is likely a bit more complex. If you're like me, you're getting your news from many different places, including Twitter and Facebook, media apps on your phone, podcasts, late-night cable TV and blogs. While my family still subscribes to a paper newspaper (two, actually) and watches the network news most nights, these sources are a much smaller percentage of our total news consumption than they used to be.

For nonprofits that are looking to advance their missions, reach new donors and enhance their reputations, the ability to navigate this complex media landscape is critical.

If you can get your story told in the right outlets in the right way, you can attract new supporters, advocate for your cause, and change minds. Without this ability, your work will be seen by far fewer people and may even be limited to people you already know.

In the past, nonprofits could get coverage by sending out generic news releases to every reporter in town and could rely on the local paper to publish grip-and-grin photos of smiling people holding large checks. But if you're still using these familiar tactics, chances are you're not getting the same results you did years ago.

Today, a successful media relations strategy requires much more than press releases and posed photos.

It involves identifying which outlets are most valuable to your organization's mission and targeting the right people within those outlets. It means positioning your expertise online. It requires monitoring multiple platforms to ensure that your mission and work is being discussed accurately.

You need to build relationships, be accessible, and offer valuable information and insights to reporters and editors. You can't do that without also listening well and understanding the nuances of news in this era.

Sadly, too many nonprofits have been slow to adapt to this new reality.

At Nonprofit Marketing Guide, I frequently hear from nonprofit communicators who wonder why their efforts to attract media coverage are falling flat. More often than not, they are getting poor results because they are still approaching media relations with the same assumptions and practices that guided this work back in the 1980s and 1990s.

Even with all of these changes, getting news coverage for your nonprofit isn't as challenging as you might think. It simply requires a new approach. It means letting go of old habits and adopting some new ideas.

That's why this book is so important.

Modern Media Relations for Nonprofits is written specifically for nonprofit communicators who are looking for practical advice for navigating this new world.

It's the first book I've seen that will help nonprofits develop effective, real-world media strategies, and execute on tactics that will get their organizations more useful media placements. You'll learn how to build better relationships with key opinion makers and also ensure that your nonprofit is prepared for the next big controversy.

I can't think of a better pair of writers to lead you through these changes. Peter and Antionette have lived on both sides of the media/nonprofit divide. Each of them has decades of newspaper and magazine bylines, in addition to experience working with and for nonprofits.

Ready to make some news?

Preface

Media relations isn't a priority for most nonprofits and foundations. And it's easy to understand why.

After all, nonprofits don't exist to grab sexy headlines. They are in business because they are working to solve complex problems and change the world. As a result, most of their resources and staff are rightfully dedicated to carrying out their missions.

But while their priorities lie elsewhere, nonprofits still need to have a well thought-out media strategy. Organizations that successfully work with reporters, editors, and opinion makers are more visible, better able to advocate for their missions, and more successful in their efforts to raise money to support their work. They also need to be prepared to respond in the unfortunate case they are inaccurately depicted in a story or on social media, or when they are at the center of a crisis or controversy.

This book is designed to help your nonprofit develop and execute on a media relations strategy. While there are a number of books that provide media relations advice, few focus on media relations through the lens of nonprofits. Nonprofits have a much different purpose than companies, politicians, or celebrities—and we've put this book together with your specific needs in mind.

This book is unique for another reason: it focuses on media relations through the lens of the current market landscape. Media has changed dramatically in recent years. And as we watch how nonprofits approach their work, we see too many examples of organizations that have been slow to adapt to these seismic industry shifts.

This why we've developed the G.R.E.A.T. approach to nonprofit media relations—Goal-oriented, Responsive, Empowered, Appealing and Targeted.

Whether you're looking to get your next event covered by the local TV station or are looking to change minds in national outlets like the Associated Press, *The Wall Street Journal* or *The New York Times*, the G.R.E.A.T. approach offers you the roadmap to success.

As professionals who have each spent more than two decades working in the media, we've witnessed this change from the inside. Peter started his career at weekly and daily community newspapers. Later, he worked as a reporter and editor at *The Chronicle of Philanthropy* where, among other things, he led its transition from a print-focused newspaper to a multi-platform news outlet that was breaking news online, on social media, and through video, podcasts, and webinars.

Antionette, meanwhile, began covering nonprofits as correspondent for *The Lexington Dispatch,* formerly *A New York Times* publication, in 1997. Although she chose a full-time career as a nonprofit professional, she still works as a news correspondent for magazines, newspapers, and blogs.

Each of us started our careers in an era when journalism was still at its peak—when local newspapers and TV stations had large budgets and actually assigned reporters to cover the nonprofits and foundations in their communities.

This era is long gone. Many of our former colleagues have been forced out of their jobs and are now working outside of the field. Those who are still working full time in newsrooms are not working on specific beats but are instead playing the role of general assignment reporters who are covering a wide array of topics (and are often being asked to file their reports in multiple mediums).

This new reality brings with it a number of challenges and opportunities for nonprofits. Gone are the days when the success of your nonprofit's public relations efforts was measured by how many times you could get a press release picked up in the local paper or how many mentions you could get on the local news. More than ever, your success depends on your ability to get the right mentions and to leverage your own networks, engage citizen journalists, and tell your own stories effectively on social media.

Many nonprofits, however, are still employing old-media public relations strategies. Communications teams are busy cranking out cookie-cutter press releases and blasting them to editors at their local newspapers, and television and radio stations, in the hope that their announcements about fundraising galas, grant awards, reports, and capital campaigns will be picked up. And they are often dismayed when the local paper ignores their announcements and instead publishes another loosely-sourced story about overhead costs and CEO salaries.

While we can't guarantee that this book will prevent your organization from showing up in one of those negative stories, if you follow the strategies we've outlined on the following pages, you will have more control over your own narrative, and you will see better results from your media outreach efforts. We will show you how to approach your relationships with reporters and editors, and how to get more mileage out of your media-relations resources.

We have also written this book with the idea that many nonprofits do not have full-time staff devoted exclusively to conducting media relations. Often, this role is just one component of a nonprofit professional's job. As a result, this book is designed to appeal to people in a number of roles. They include:

Communications and public relations staff. Whether you're new in your role or a veteran looking for advice on how to navigate the new media landscape, this book is packed with strategies and tips that will help your organization get more coverage and build better relationships with the media.

Executive leadership. Although many top nonprofit executives display a level of confidence with public speaking, media relations often require a different level of interaction and preparation. You will learn how to navigate those differences with a concentration on getting the best coverage possible. It will also help you more effectively manage your communications team.

Board members. Board members are drilled to prepare an "elevator speech," which they can share in a brief conversation that communicates the organization's mission, values, and purpose. However, we have found that few are prepared for media questions or inquiries during a special event, in the midst of an executive transition, or during a dreaded crisis situation. This guide can assist board members to remain calm and confident while approaching media, or while being approached for an interview or statement.

Program staff. Even if you are not identified as the primary person responsible for communications, this guide will help you prepare for any level of media interaction. In many cases, we have found that reporters tire of interviewing the same person (e.g., president or PR person) and will ask for someone closer to the story.

No matter your role, we're thankful that you've chosen to invest in learning more about effective media relations. Your mission might not revolve around getting positive headlines, but by successfully navigating this new media landscape, your organization will stand a better chance of achieving its mission.

Introduction

This book serves as your guide for building and carrying out an effective modern media relations strategy. While there are plenty of other books that offer instruction on media relations, this one is written specifically for those who work for nonprofits and foundations.

The path to a successful modern media strategy will be different for each nonprofit. We recognize that for some reading this book, much of this information could be brand new. With that in mind we want to introduce an easy to remember acronym for your Modern Media strategy: G.R.E.A.T, which stands for Goal Oriented, Responsive, Empowered, Appealing and Targeted. This framework will be a guide for new nonprofit professionals as well as those who have experience but are looking to improve their modern media strategy.

PART 1

The Basics

CHAPTER 1

Understanding Modern Media

Many of us don't have to stretch our memories to recall the days when local newspapers and TV stations had beefy reporting staffs and large news holes to fill. Back then, getting your story told in a national media outlet would bring your nonprofit serious cache—and a huge audience.

But those days are over.

Today's newsrooms are a shell of what they once were—the result of a dramatic shakeup that has transformed the journalism world. The explosion of the internet—and later social media and smartphones—has shattered the business model for local and national media outlets, and changed the way we consume information.

Most of us no longer read newspapers that are plopped on our doorsteps every morning or build our evening schedules around the 6 o'clock news. We get our information elsewhere, often through 'news' sources that conform to our interests and worldview. Instead of watching Cronkite, Rather or Brokaw, we read blogs, tune in to conservative or liberal cable news, and scroll our Facebook feeds for content that validates our opinions.

These changes are dramatically altering the way nonprofits should approach getting coverage for their work. For many nonprofits today, getting their story told on a well-regarded blog—or even linked to by an influencer on Twitter—can have a bigger impact than a story that's picked up in the local newspaper.

Today, effective media relations is no longer about generating press releases and making pitches to a handful of trusted outlets. It requires nuance, and a willingness to try new approaches.

In some ways, media relations today is more rewarding, and the opportunities for reaching your key audiences are more plentiful.

But it's by no means easy.

To better understand these new phenomena, it's helpful to look closer at how some key industries in the media are changing:

Traditional Print and Digital Media
(Newspapers, Magazines, and Trade and Business Magazines)

It's getting harder to attract the attention of traditional newspaper and magazine reporters. First off, there are a lot fewer of them than there were just a few years ago. In 2015 alone, the number of newsroom jobs dropped by 10.4 percent, down to 32,900 full-time journalists at nearly 1,400 U.S. dailies, according to the American Society of News Editors. That's a loss of 3,800 jobs in just one year (Newsonomics: The halving of America's daily newsrooms, Ken Doctor 2015). And that drop follows several years of similar declines in U.S. newsrooms.

Not surprisingly, there are fewer reporters covering nonprofits than at any time in our memories. Anecdotally, our friends who remain in the reporting business say they are stretched further than ever. They often have to crank out multiple stories each day on a variety of topics simply because there are fewer hands on deck to get out the next day's edition. In many cases, they are working for conglomerates that are headquartered far from the city where they work, and forced to face quotas and standards that didn't exist even a few years ago.

In some cities—including what were, until recently, "two-newspaper towns"—daily newspapers have gone out of business completely. Others have cut back to printing only a few days a week. A handful more, like the *Christian Science Monitor*, have abandoned their daily print formats in favor of digital-only editions.

But even those that are printing seven days a week are producing much thinner editions than they once were (often by shrinking the width of the paper itself, cutting the number of pages, and eliminating entire sections of coverage). Today, nearly every "paper" is now primarily focused on delivering news online—and reporters must now face 24-hour demand for news with video feeds and Twitter promotions related to news stories. Chapter Eight: "More than Words" covers how the contribution of additional materials like graphics, video footage, and photos have impacted, and provides examples of what other nonprofits are doing to enhance news stories.

Today, news still travels, but it is by way of satellites and across wireless networks. Newspapers and magazines have learned to stay relevant by embracing video and podcasts, website development, crowdsourcing, hyper-local reporting, and online news production.

But even as they evolve, most daily newspapers are a shadow of what they were back when Robert Redford and Dustin Hoffman were bringing down Richard Nixon in *All The President's Men*—or even when Mark Ruffalo and Rachel McAdams were crusading against the Boston Archdiocese in *Spotlight*.

It saddens us as former print reporters. But, nonetheless, it's the reality.

Broadcast Media
(Radio and Television)

In "Revolutionizing the Newsroom: How Online and Mobile Technologies Have Changed Broadcast Journalism," Nicole Chadwick interviewed 13 local and network broadcast journalists to determine how the industry has changed during the internet age. She asked the following questions:

- How is your job affected by online and mobile news? Are you required to have a web presence for your job?
- What is the greatest change to the newsroom since the introduction of online and mobile news?
- What's next? Will there still be traditional newscasts in the future?

The answers were revealing—and provided a number of lessons to nonprofits, detailed in the section below on citizen journalism.

Citizen Journalism
(Social Media, Blogs, and Podcasts)

Online and mobile technologies are transforming the broadcasting business. Just like print journalists, broadcast reporters are having to multitask. Chadwick notes in her research that: "Online and mobile technologies play an increasingly prominent role in television newsrooms, particularly on the local level" (Chadwick

2014). In her study, she emphasized the importance of having an online component and an on-air news broadcast, primarily because breaking news no longer waits for a television or radio broadcast. "Many of the local journalists explained their stations have gone 'web first,' which demonstrates how much the industry has changed from having only on-air broadcasts in the 1990s, to web pages for most stations, to interactive websites and mobile apps, which have become standard for many stations across the country" (Chadwick 2014).

Reporters with a social media following add value to networks. Did you know that following a reporter and media personality on their professional Facebook page, Instagram, SnapChat, or Twitter helps them professionally? Chadwick gives examples in her report, writing that (Chadwick 2014).

The most influential contributor to the changing field of journalism today is its audience. The emergence of blogs, podcasts, streaming video, and other web-related innovations, has led to the emergence of so-called citizen journalism. Today, anyone with a smartphone can capture and publish video of breaking news—and anyone with a working internet connection can publish their own commentary.

Citizen journalism has become a crucial part of many existing news networks' coverage, and independent news sites have been launched to accommodate this new wave of tech-savvy, news-hungry citizen advocacy.

Michael Nigro, award-winning filmmaker and Emmy-nominated writer-director, credits citizen journalism with delivering the most powerful social justice movements over the past decade in "Let's All Commit Acts of Citizen Journalism" (Huffington Post

Blog March, 2016). "Having witnessed the news of their lives being dismissed or ignored, more and more people have put their bodies on the line, their ink on the page and their images on the web. With defiance, tenacity and boots-on-the-ground bravery—and often with little or no financial backing—independent and citizen journalists are utilizing tools of the digital age to change the conversation at a grassroots level" (Nigro 2016).

What does this mean for nonprofits?

Hyper-local coverage. Citizen journalism has paved the way for hyper-local coverage of important issues. In the United States, many newsrooms have been downsized in recent years to cut costs. Citizen journalists, and citizen journalism websites, could potentially help fill the void left by the departure of so many professional reporters. Unfortunately, this is not yet the case in many communities—and there are fears that the media might be ceding its role as a watchdog to local government.

A new level of advocacy. Independent fact-checking blogs and independent news criticism sites now challenge the authority of traditional media and offer an alternative.

A citizen journalist or advocacy journalist is often free of the constraints and bureaucracy of a professional newsroom. However, it also means that these "reporters" do not typically have editors to help fact-check or oversee the final product. As a result, there is some controversy over the term "citizen journalism" because many professional journalists believe that only a trained journalist can understand the complexities and ethics involved in reporting the news. However, for a nonprofit, finding someone who has a following that shares the same values can result in a more meaningful dialogue and better coverage of your work.

"Think back to even just a few years ago when issues like income inequality, divestment from fossil fuels, student debt, the prison industrial complex, global warming and Black Lives Matter were barely a sound bite within the national dialogue," Nigro writes. "The trees were, in fact, falling in the forest but it is thanks to independent and citizen journalists that the public actually heard the sound" (Nigro 2016).

Dangerous territory. Citizen journalism has its pitfalls. It can spiral out of control quickly and open the nonprofit to media attention for which it is not prepared. Such was the case with the nonprofit Invisible Children and a controversial video campaign called Kony 2012. The small nonprofit was thrust into the center of a media firestorm when it released a short documentary video online about Joseph Kony, the notorious militia leader in northern Uganda. The video, which was shared initially by Invisible Children's supporters and later by celebrities such as Rihanna and Bill Gates, garnered a whopping 120 million views in just five days. At the time, the technology website Mashable named it the most viral video ever.

But Invisible Children was not prepared for the flood of media attention that followed. Critics claimed the nonprofit had exaggerated Kony's crimes. Other advocacy organizations accused Invisible Children of oversimplifying a complex issue and questioned how the organization managed its money. Less than two weeks after "Kony 2012" became Invisible Children's viral sensation, Jason Russell, the executive who narrated the video, had a mental breakdown.

The lesson is clear: as you court attention, you must be prepared for both praise and criticism. As our world becomes ever more connected—and as citizen advocacy continues to grow—it is important for nonprofits to understand both the benefits and pitfalls of courting citizen advocacy.

CHAPTER 2

Understanding Journalism

We open this chapter with a few basic journalism definitions that you will come across in this book. These definitions will also help you as you navigate day-to-day communication with the media.

Common Jargon Used by Reporters and Producers

Beats. An area assigned to a reporter for regular coverage. Many newspapers have reporters who cover nonprofit stories. This would be considered the nonprofit "beat." Some other common beats for reporters who cover issues that matter to the nonprofit world include health, arts, and religion.

Embargo. Providing information or an announcement to a reporter ahead of its formal release. Under the terms of an embargo, the journalist is allowed to gather information and conduct interviews but they are not allowed to make the report public until an agreed-upon time. This gives the reporter the opportunity to compile a more complete report, but gives you—as the source—the opportunity to coordinate when the information is made public.

Feature story. A story emphasizing the human or entertaining aspects of a situation.

No comment. No comment is a phrase used as a response to journalistic inquiries when the person declines to answer questions. Journalists will note in stories when the respondent refuses to comment. Typically "not available for comment" implies that the reporter was unable to contact the person before their deadline or the person did not respond to correspondence.

Nut graph. Nut graphs are paragraphs that often appear early in a news story — typically in the second or third paragraph — and set the context for what follows. They can be full paragraphs, short sentences, or something in between. But no matter the length, a good nut graph offers a clear roadmap to what makes the story important.

Examples of nut graphs can be found in Chapter Three, in the section on press releases.

Off the record. Describes information or materials offered to the reporter in confidence. If the reporter accepts information with this understanding, it cannot be used unless they are able to get the information confirmed by other sources. In such cases, it is expected that the reporter will not divulge who provided them with the original information. Sometimes, reporters will not accept a request to go off the record, and they are under no legal obligation to do so after you have shared the information (so be careful). Anything shared with a journalist—verbally or otherwise—should be treated as on the record unless both the journalist and the source agree to go off the record.

Op-ed page. An abbreviation for the page opposite the editorial page. The page is frequently devoted to opinion columns and related illustrations.

Press release. A written document that announces news to the media, with the goal of having them use the information in the announcement in their reporting. Also called a "news release".

Source. A person, record, document, or event that provides the information needed for the story.

Stringer or correspondent. Typically not a regular staff member, but a freelancer who is paid per story or by the number of words written.

Tip. The information passed to a reporter, often in confidence.

Broadcast-Related Terms

Close up. A camera shot of the face of the subject that dominates the frame so that little background is visible.

Cover shot. A longer camera shot usually placed at the beginning of a sequence to establish the place or location.

Cue. A signal in a script, word, or gesture to begin or to stop.

Soundbite. A short clip usually taken from a longer quote. Also referred to as a "teaser."

Are You Newsworthy?

A lot of nonprofits believe that just because they are having an event, it deserves news coverage. But do not be surprised if a producer or reporter asks you to tell them what makes your story newsworthy.

What makes a story newsworthy often seems objective to journalists but can be gauged by the following characteristics:

Human interest. Human-interest stories are where nonprofits can really shine. These stories often disregard the main rules of newsworthiness. Human-interest stories appeal to emotion. These are great fillers for media outlets on slow news days. Television news programs often hold a place for a humorous or quirky story at the end of the show to finish on a feel-good note. Newspapers often have a dedicated area for "offbeat" or human interest items.

Impact. Whether it is a walk for a cure that encompasses five city blocks or a large number of people being displaced from their homes, the more involved the event, the more newsworthy it is. Try pitching a story of data based on impact.

Localized. For local news outlets, stories that happen near the audience of the media source will have more significance. The closer the story is to home, the more newsworthy it is. If you are working with a national nonprofit agency, consider finding local people and pitching their stories to media outlets nearby.

Timeliness. Is it current? News often needs to be told quickly if it is going to be told at all. If it happened today, it could be considered news. If the same thing happened last week, it could be deemed as no longer newsworthy.

Prominence. Famous, notable, and extraordinary people often receive more press coverage. On a local level, local politicians and civic leaders are often considered prominent, though they might not have prominence outside of that community.

Significance. The number of people affected by the story is an important consideration among editors and reporters when they make decisions about coverage. A flood displacing hundreds of families will have a broader reach than a flood that displaces one family.

Oddity. If something is unusual, shocking, or bizarre, this alone could make a story newsworthy.

The Basics of Journalism Ethics

Even though the media world is changing quickly, most reputable journalists still adhere to the same ethical rules that guided the profession for much of the 20th century. As a result, if you handle media relations for your nonprofit, it is important to understand the rules that govern professional journalism. These rules might appear quaint in this age of partisan cable networks, fake news, and opinion-based websites. But, believe it or not, most news organizations are still working under the idea that journalists should be responsible with the information they gather, and the sources with whom they work. Ultimately, these rules are designed to protect you because they encourage journalists to be fair and unbiased.

Knowing these rules can help your organization get the coverage it deserves, especially if you are dealing with a reporter who is documenting a sensitive issue related to your organization or its mission. It can also help you set the right expectations when you do something as simple as offer complimentary admission to reporters at your annual fundraising dinner.

If you are new to media relations—or you are an experienced hand that needs a refresher—we recommend taking some time to review the code of ethics from the Society of Professional Journalists, which should provide you with the background you need to understand the rules of the road. At the highest level, the rules are simple. Journalists are obligated to perform the following:

- Seek and report the truth
- Be fair to their sources

- Act as the public's watchdog
- Avoid any conflicts of interest that would jeopardize their ability to report objectively.

How does this code apply to the nonprofit world? Here's a true/false test that should help you navigate some common situations that crop up for nonprofits dealing with the media.

Journalism Ethics True or False

True or false: We advertise in the newspaper; we deserve positive stories.

False. Most news organizations have a bright line between their advertising departments and their newsrooms—for good reason. Journalists are not supposed to let the fact that advertisers spend money on their outlets sway the news they report. Your advertisement buys you the opportunity to spread your own message in the space you reserved, and it needs to be clear to readers or viewers that it is a paid advertisement. Placing an ad guarantees you nothing beyond the ad.

True or false: I should expect to review a story about my organization before it is published.

False. Responsible news organizations do not hand over the controls to the subjects they are covering. However, that does not mean you are out of luck if you want to make sure a reporter is getting the facts correct. Some reporters will agree to read direct quotes to you for accuracy or review facts and figures before publication. If it is a reported news story, they have no obligation to clear any information they gather with you ahead of time. Reporters who value accuracy will be sure to double-check facts with their sources. In some cases, newspaper stories may appear online before they are printed, and this may give you an opportunity to read the story and contact the reporter with quick corrections.

True or false: It is acceptable for me to limit photography of my programs, especially if my organization works with children or vulnerable populations.

True. Although you might feel pressure to allow a news organization to record or photograph the people you serve, they also have obligations to protect those who cannot give consent or who are in vulnerable positions. Reputable news organizations will respect your rules if you work with vulnerable populations. If there are situations where your organization might want to have its programs photographed or recorded by the media, you might consider creating a process for getting consent from the children or those you serve, and making it clear to the media organization who has agreed to be photographed.

But while it is acceptable to ask for these conditions, it should not be assumed that a journalist will know what you consider off limits. Legally, a journalist doesn't need consent to talk to a source or take a photograph. As a result, says Chad Bowman, a partner at law firm Levine Sullivan Koch & Schulz in Washington D.C., it's important to work out the ground rules ahead of time.

True or false: We do not have to share our IRS forms with the media.

False. Because your nonprofit's revenues are exempt from taxes and are generated through the generosity of donors, your IRS Form 990s are considered public record. Refusing to provide them could get you in legal trouble. It could also raise red flags with inquiring reporters who are ethically bound to serve as public watchdogs. Many organizations make it very easy for reporters and the public to access their 990s. Some nonprofits go a step further and publicly release their audited financial statements or make them available online.

True or false: The story about my nonprofit contains inaccurate information. I should demand a correction.

True. Reputable journalism organizations will acknowledge mistakes and correct them quickly and prominently. If you see a mistake, you should say something to the reporter or editor responsible for it. Chapter 12 provides advice on how to ask for a correction and what to do when a reporter gets your story wrong.

True or false: Our nonprofit was portrayed negatively in a story. We should demand a retraction.

This is false, most of the time. If the story is factually true and is an example of a news organization holding you accountable for failing to deliver on your mission or abusing your resources, you are probably out of luck. You need to look no further than the 2016 investigative pieces on the Wounded Warrior Project—which questioned the high-profile organization's spending policies—to see how the news media handles its role as a watchdog of nonprofits. However, if the story is based on false information or shoddy reporting, you have every right to stand up for your organization and demand accountability. Journalists, like doctors, are supposed to "do no harm." This means they should not unfairly target those who are acting responsibly.

True or false: I can offer a reporter free admission to our annual dinner.

True. Do not be surprised, though, if they refuse and pay their own way instead. Some news organizations let reporters enter paid events for free if they are there to cover the event. Others will choose to pay the admission fee for their reporters because they do not want their reporters to feel indebted to the organizations they cover. Even if they accept free admission, they should stop short of accepting other freebies, like travel costs or meals.

As you can see, there are a number of gray areas. Regardless of how an individual reporter responds in certain situations, it is important to remember that most journalists are trying to work within a set of professional rules. As you develop relationships, it is okay to ask questions about how they (their news organization) approach each of these gray areas. By showing an interest in how they approach their work and maintain their objectivity, you are sending them a message that you respect what they do and are interested in the same goals. In turn, this will help yield respectful and fair coverage of your own work.

It's crucial to remember, though, that while journalists have a code of ethics and are trained to be fair and impartial in their reporting, "this code is not considered to be law," Bowman said.

Journalists actually have wide legal leeway in gathering information. Any time you speak to reporters, or share information with them, you should know that it's possible that your words or information could end up in their reporting.

If you seek to provide information on background or off the record, make sure that you work out your terms up front and that both sides are clear on those terms.

"When you are dealing with a reporter, particularly about something sensitive, negotiate access," Bowman says. "Any ambiguity is going to be considered fair game."

We'll explore more about legal issues later in this book, but it's important to know some of the basic ground rules up front to avoid headaches later.

CHAPTER 3

What's in Your Toolkit?

When most people think of a media relations strategy, they often focus almost exclusively on earned media—that is, earning placements in newspapers, magazines, TV news programs, radio news segments and the like. Generating earned media offers your organization an opportunity to spread its message through a trusted third party. Such placements are incredibly valuable—and we devote a lot of this book to helping you achieve these placements.

But it is important to note that earned media isn't your only option for spreading your message. In fact, you might want to think about how you can stretch your earned media efforts into other arenas. To get the most bang for your buck—and to maximize your time—every time you pursue an earned media placement, think about how you can hit the TRIFECTA of earned, paid, and owned media. To understand how this works, let's dig a bit deeper into the three components of the Trifecta:

Earned media. Journalism in its truest form refers to publicly gained news stories from an independent source—other than paid advertising—including television, newspapers, magazines, podcasts and radio.

Paid media. Advertising that promotes content in order to drive earned media as well as direct traffic to owned media properties. Your nonprofit can take out ads in traditional media, record public service announcements, or place targeted ads on social media sites like Facebook, Twitter and LinkedIn. Social media advertising has become an increasingly popular choice for nonprofits because it offers a number of advantages over traditional ads. Not only are social media ads fairly low in cost, they allow advertisers to target ads to specific demographics and get almost instantaneous reporting on who is engaging with the ad.

Owned media. Owned media is any property that you control and is unique to your brand. Some of the most common examples are websites, online newsrooms, newsletters, annual reports, blogs, social media, and any printed materials that your organization publishes.

Owned media can:
- Amplify your earned and paid media strategies
- Communicate your brand
- Challenge stereotypes or unwanted images about your work
- Present empowered messages
- Demonstrate thought leadership on important topics.

While earned media is an important component of your overall media-relations strategy, it's important to make sure you also pay attention to paid and owned media. This will help you reach your key audiences on your own terms—and can help you counteract poor or negative coverage in earned media outlets. The important thing to remember that each of these outlets will reach a different audience.

For example, Antionette worked with a community college to launch a campaign to attract non-traditional students and more minority men. The community college paid more than $30,000 for an elaborate advertising campaign that included radio, print ads and billboards [paid media]—which it considered to be an important investment. But the agency's paid media effort wasn't coordinated with its earned media strategy, which focused on pitching stories to publications about the accomplishments of the women's volleyball team (no minority men and traditional students), and its international scholars program (minority men but from other countries and traditional students). Meanwhile, the college also failed to make its website [owned media] reflect what it was desperately trying to communicate.

After Antionette assessed its communications efforts, she recommended to the organization that it take a different approach. Ultimately, it chose to pull back funding from its advertising campaign and to be more strategic with their owned media. This decision drew cheers from the communications staff, which had been pushing for years to improve its website. We're not saying don't invest in advertising, just be sure you are investing wisely and think about reinforcing the message across all three components of the trifecta.

Press Releases

Now that we've explored the differences between earned, paid, and owned media, let's take a deeper dive into some of the components of your earned media toolkit.

Perhaps the most common tool for the media relations professional is the press release. A press release is an effective tool for sharing news with reporters and editors.. Press releases should be written in third-person with objective data and key facts about the program or idea you're introducing. Here are a few press release basics to keep in mind:

- Write professionally but stay away from using industry jargon that readers may not understand.
- Write out acronyms the first time you use them; use abbreviations later.
- Remember that your press release is ultimately for your audience. If that audience doesn't understand it, then you are completely missing the point.
- Use a press release to provide essential information about newsworthy announcements (e.g., launch of a new program, an agency or individual professional milestone, a new grant, or announcing an event).
- Keep them short. Some of the most effective releases are kept to just one page.
- Include your press contact's email and cell number prominently at the top of your release. Since many reporters work on deadline news stories after regular business hours, provide an after-hours number, if possible.
- Include boilerplate language about your organization and its mission.

Good releases go beyond the basics and help show reporters why what you're announcing is important to their readers or viewers. To earn attention it's typically not enough to simply write a release announcing a new program. Instead, the release should explain—clearly and prominently—why this new program is important and what it hopes to accomplish.

To achieve this goal, it's important for your release to contain a "nut graph" that explains why your announcement is worth covering.

Nut graphs can be full paragraphs, short sentences, or something in between. But no matter the length, a good nut graph offers a clear roadmap to what makes the story important.

If you can quickly and concisely identify and articulate why the story you are pitching is important, you stand a better chance of convincing the reporter that it is a story worth telling. This is your opportunity to give the reporter a clear news hook and for you to help place the story in a context that advances your organization's goals.

But how do you find that context?

Here are five questions that you can ask before you write your release that will help you determine how you should frame your nut graph:

1. What is different about this release?

Let's use a common topic for a news release as an example: announcing a new executive director. The fact that you are announcing a new executive director for your organization isn't different. Every organization hires a new director from time to time. But the person you are hiring usually brings something new to the table. Perhaps she is the first woman to lead an arts organization in your city, or he is the first graduate of your program to come back and lead it.

If you can identify something different that might help your announcement stand out, your nut graph becomes easier. Here's an example:

"Jones, who is the organization's seventeenth director, is the first woman to lead a major arts organization in Gotham City."

2. Is this part of a larger trend?

Let's say you are having a hard time identifying what's different with your announcement. In that case, maybe you can focus on how it connects to a larger trend.

Reporters are always looking for trends, but because they don't work for nonprofits, they might not recognize that your announcement of a new program, partnership, or major gift is actually reflective of a larger trend. By pointing out a trend in your nut graph, you're helping the reporter find a hook for the story and showing how your organization is part of a larger movement.

Example: "The new program is part of a growing trend among nonprofits that are partnering with local community foundations to track and measure progress toward improving adult literacy rates. Similar programs in cities including Detroit and Pittsburgh are already showing great promise in addressing this important issue."

3. What is the impact?

Impact is a buzzword in the nonprofit world, and for good reason. If you can identify what impact your announcement will have on the community it serves or a problem you're trying to solve, you have a ready-made news hook—and a nut graph that almost writes itself.

Example: "With this grant from Vandelay Industries, the Kramer Center will be able to provide housing assistance to 300 families that otherwise would be unable to afford rents in the neighborhood."

4. Is it timely?

Perhaps your release helps address an issue that is particularly timely or connects to a larger event in the news. Identifying a connection to something current can help give you the hook you need for your nut graph.

Example: "At a time when many local workers have lost their jobs due to the recent recession, this new program offers career training and placement services that are otherwise difficult to afford."

5. Can someone learn from it?

For some outlets, "news you can use" is in high demand. Rather than simple reporting on an announcement, many outlets are looking for content that helps readers or viewers learn something they can apply to their own lives.

Your nonprofit, for example, might have developed a way to create cool videos on a small budget or how to partner with organizations to purchase supplies at a lower cost than you could on your own. Pitching these developments as stories that can help teach other nonprofit leaders or businesses how to be more effective could help you land stories and do some good in the process.

Example: "The new partnership is the result of months of deliberate planning and negotiations, and provides a roadmap for other organizations looking to manage their costs responsibly."

For more examples of Press Releases visit our online Modern Media Relations Resource Center at turn-two.co

Crafting Statements, Op-Eds and Editorials

Op-eds are another valuable tool. A well-placed op-ed can help your nonprofit call attention to an important issue or change minds about a controversial topic. Unlike reported news stories, op-eds are opinion pieces that are written by those who aren't on the staff of a newspaper, magazine or website. They offer outside voices the opportunity to express opinions and share ideas in their own words. Traditionally, they appear opposite the editorial page (hence the name, op-ed), which is where the newspaper's editorial board expresses its opinion on important issues.

While newspapers don't quite carry the same influence as they once did, op-eds can nonetheless be valuable tools for advocacy-minded organizations and groups that are looking to raise awareness about a problem or issue. In fact, one could argue that op-eds have more influence than ever.

That's because a published op-ed not only appears in the newspaper, it also appears online, which gives your nonprofit the opportunity to point to it on its own site, in blog posts, and through its social media channels.

But, as is the case with pitching stories, it's a challenge to get news outlets to run your opinion piece.

Newspapers and other outlets typically only have the resources and space to run a limited number of op-eds. As result, competition for these pieces can be fierce.

So how can you increase your odds of getting published?

Here are 10 tips that can help you get your op-ed to the top of the pile:

1. Be Targeted

   Before you begin the process of writing and pitching an op-ed, spend some time thinking about which outlet or outlets are of greatest value in terms of reaching your target audiences. If you're a locally focused nonprofit, that will likely be your local newspaper. But it could also be an outlet that reaches a certain demographic, a trade publication, or a website.

2. Get to Know the Publication

Once you've identified the outlet you're looking to target, spend some time reading its opinion pages. Get a sense of the type of pieces it typically runs and its preferred tone. Reach out to the opinion editor to inquire about its editorial guidelines and, if possible, discuss potential topics or ideas. This will help you avoid sending a blind pitch—and it could end up giving you the intel you need to draft a piece that will appeal to that editor.

3. Understand That You're Writing on Spec

It takes time to write an effective op-ed. But you have to invest that time with the understanding that your piece might not be accepted. As a result, you will be working without any guarantee that your piece will get published. Ultimately, you need to invest that time in writing a strong enough piece for it to get considered, so resist the urge to cut corners. If you can't afford to take the time to produce a high-quality piece, your chances of success are low.

4. Don't Be Afraid to Ghostwrite

Newspapers typically won't accept op-eds that are written by a director of communications or spokesperson. Your piece will need to come from an expert in the issue you're discussing—most likely your top executive or another official within your organization. Often, these folks don't have hours to devote to writing an op-ed on spec. So you'll likely need to draft the piece yourself under another person's byline—or hire an outside ghostwriter to work with the expert to create a strong draft.

5. Make It About Your Mission

   Most news outlets will not publish op-eds that are promotional in nature. As a result, a piece about why people should support your organization or attend your fundraising dinner isn't likely to fly. Instead, you need to focus on an issue or problem. Think about your mission and what you're trying to accomplish and develop topics that build off of your mission. If you're working on anti-poverty initiatives, for instance, consider writing about the root causes of poverty or effective programs.

6. Find Creative Ways to Position Your Point of View

   Identify a creative angle or framework for your piece to increase your chances of success. For example, if you work for a nonprofit that specializes in early-childhood education, you could offer advice to a newly elected official on how to address that issue. You can also look for opportunities to offer insights into new research or explore the implications of a new report or Census data that relates to your cause.

7. Illustrate With Real Stories

   While it might be tempting to load your op-ed with data, keep in mind that people are more likely to remember human stories than they are hard figures. As a result, try to find ways to incorporate anecdotes and stories into your piece to help give it added punch.

8. Keep It Short

   Most outlets aren't looking for lengthy opinion pieces. They expect writers to keep their opinion submissions short—often in the neighborhood of 800 to 1,000 words, or less. Newspapers, of course, have limited space, so they need to fit as much as they can into their limited real estate. But even though the web offers unlimited space, attention spans are short. So your pieces should be, as well. Jennifer Finney Boyer of The New York Times recommends that if you send a piece that's longer than what the outlet usually publishes, that you include in your cover letter that the piece can be cut.

9. Be Ready for Dissenting Views

If your piece discusses a controversial topic, be prepared for a negative response from some readers. Your piece might prompt nasty online comments or an angry letter to the editor. Be ready for blowback—and develop a plan for how you'll respond. This is often a good problem to have, since it means that your piece was not only published, but it also struck a nerve. But have a plan in place for how you'd like to engage those who disagree.

10. Remember to Repurpose

If you are fortunate enough to get your piece published, make sure you have a plan for promoting it on your website and through your social-media channels—and freely encourage your board members and other supporters to help you spread the word. Since you wrote the piece, you might even be able to cross-post it to your blog or edit it to submit to other outlets. And if it doesn't get accepted, make sure your time and effort isn't wasted. Use the piece in your own channels or pitch it somewhere else.

CHAPTER 4

Helping Reporters Find You

You don't have to rely solely on your own pitches to get your organization quoted or cited in the media. Sometimes, you can get coverage by connecting with journalists when they are looking to find an expert as they report their own stories.

Journalists are often looking for experts and sources for stories they're already working on—and they often struggle to find new voices to round out their reporting. But the challenge is making sure your organization gets the reporter's call when they need a source in your subject area.

One way is to sign up for an online service in which reporters and bloggers solicit sources for their stories. These services offer nonprofits a chance to get daily queries from writers who are working on assigned stories.

It should be noted that responding to these queries won't guarantee you coverage—reporters tend to get a flood of responses when they use these services. But there are steps you can take to help get your response to the top of the pile.

The best-known service is HARO—or Help a Reporter Out. Three times every day, HARO delivers an email to sources that includes dozens of queries from reporters who are looking for experts. The reporters provide descriptions of the stories they are working on and the type of expertise they are seeking. Each query includes a link where potential sources can reply and say why they should be considered as an expert for the story.

While HARO is the biggest and most recognized service, it is far from the only game in town. Other options include:

ProfNet – A service of PR Newswire, ProfNet is built for public relations professionals who want to find opportunities to pitch their organizations to journalists. Users set up an online profile and set preferences for the types of queries they are interested in seeing. You are also able to set up your own online profile to establish your credentials and can pitch journalists on your expertise to help them quickly find sources during breaking news stories and events.

SourceBottle – Like the other services, SourceBottle sends emails with reporter queries to potential sources. It also includes a searchable online database of active queries, which makes it easy for time-strapped PR professionals to find queries that line up with their areas of expertise.

PitchRate – Offers an opportunity to search queries online. Many of the queries are from bloggers and websites that are looking for experts to comment or provide written materials for publication.

These resources can be useful to help position experts to reporters who are already working on stories. But they aren't for everyone.

In addition to the volume of responses many reporters get when they post queries, many of the queries themselves aren't a great fit for nonprofits. Many of the posts focus on stories related to self-help, finance, or national topics.

But if your nonprofit works on health-related issues—or has an expertise in topics such as education or the environment—you are likely to find some queries that connect with your mission. Still, you'll need to be patient and wade through quite a few requests before you find one worth your time.

If you do choose to respond to a query, it's important to take a few steps to ensure that you're providing the reporter something useful. We have posted our share of requests on ProfNet and HARO, and we can tell you what helped get our attention when we were looking at responses from sources.

How to Respond When a Reporter Contacts You

Your response should:

- Speak directly to what the reporter is looking for; reporters who post on these sites already have a story assignment in hand and are often looking to fill a specific hole in their reporting. If they need an expert in early childhood education to offer advice to parents who are sending their first child to kindergarten for the first time, don't use the query as an opportunity to suggest a story on problems with statewide testing.

- Establish your expertise. Make it very clear why you (or a person at your organization) are the best person to speak about the topic. Talk about your background, what you do, and perhaps even offer a short anecdote that establishes you as someone who knows the topic well.

- Be prompt. Reporters often use services like HARO because they need someone quickly. Journalism is a deadline-driven business. Pay attention to the reporter's deadline and be sure that you are able to have someone available to comment quickly, as needed.

- Include tips and quotable material. While your response should be succinct, it should also be specific. If the reporter is looking for advice on a particular topic, include a handful of tips that they can plug into the story, if they're short on time. You can even provide a useful quote that can be attributed to you or another person at your organization.

- Provide contact information. Your goal is to make it as easy as possible for the reporter to include your expertise in their story. To help the process along, provide your phone number and email address. You should also include a link to your organization's website (in case the reporter wants to do some quick research on who you are) and any relevant social media links (such as your Twitter handle or Facebook page).

Keep in mind that you can do all of the above and still not make the cut. Like other PR tactics, services like HARO are competitive. A reporter might only have time or space to include one response in their story. As a result, the reporter has to leave out a number of legitimate and credible sources.

Being smart about crafting your responses will increase your chances of getting results.

Developing an Efficient Online Newsroom

Online newsrooms can save you time and make it easy for media sources to get high-quality images, quotes, and data. An online newsroom can also save you the time and effort of having to email journalists important information. Think beyond the traditional string of press releases and old-fashioned press kits that organizations used to mail to media outlets or provide at the door of an event.

Your online newsroom can be a simple page on your website that includes:

- Press Releases organized by topic
- An RSS (Rich Site Summary) feed of your announcements and releases
- High Resolution Photos
- High Quality Videos
- Executive summaries of research
- IRS Form 990s
- Annual Reports
- Biographical information for staff, thought leaders and speaker bios

Each year the TEKGROUP conducts an Online Newsroom Survey Report highlighting the expectations that journalists have for organizations and their online newsrooms, and then they provide a free report that nonprofits find useful to monitor this trend.

TEKGROUP recommends that online newsrooms include more than just a list of press releases (although having a few of those are important). Some organizations have converted their online newsrooms into interactive and social-media-enabled communications centers that are automatically updated. Other organizations have created a "dark" site that allows them to have a private store of communications materials and statements ready to go for crisis communications efforts.

Cindy Olnick, Director of Communications of the Los Angeles Conservancy, says online newsrooms are a vital tool for organizations that want to stand out to today's reporters. "Deadlines are faster because reporters have to get information online before anyone else does," said Olnick. "They are responsible for more than just the copy. We find ourselves providing more content such as images, and copy for tweets and Facebook posts."

Olnick's organization has focused on creating an online newsroom that includes information that can be easily shared on social media . It also ensures that the site is bubbling with information during major events. After these events it shares images on its webpage and shares Dropbox links with its targeted press list so they can easily access and download images for their stories and social media postings.

Why do journalists love online newsrooms?

- They can access important information before, during and after an event which helps them meet deadlines.
- They can quickly confirm important details about your organization and reduce errors.
- They can quickly access videos, social media posts and high-resolution images, which helps them meet their publisher/ stations' demands for layered content.

These are just a few examples of what you should have in your basic toolkit. Later we will talk about some more advanced techniques for making your media relations toolkit G.R.E.A.T.

CHAPTER 5

Making Your
Media Strategy G.R.E.A.T

Now that you we've covered the basics, you're ready to get started with improving your nonprofit's presence in the media.

Even with the right tools, true success comes with having the right media relations strategy.

And to help you ensure that you're accomplishing this goal, here's a tool you can use to help measure your progress—using the acronym G.R.E.A.T.

To achieve ultimate success, your media relations strategy should be:

Goal-Oriented. A great strategy starts with clear goals. But many nonprofits do not take the time to align their media relations activities with their organization's goals. Targeted media relations begins with understanding what your organization is actually looking to accomplish short-term and long-term. As a result, it's important that you not only have a strong understanding of your nonprofit's mission, but also have key strategic priorities to support that mission.

Responsive. Effective media relations isn't about pitching. It's about building strong relationships with journalists—and being responsive to their needs. Has your organization planned ahead and created the resources and structure to capitalize on breaking news, identify and act on trends in data and arising community needs, and handle potential crises? Are you equipped to quickly answer questions and respond to media requests? Do you have a page on your website for reporters to find information and connect with the appropriate people on your team? Being responsive is not something that you figure out along the way. It requires preparation and the ability to present your nonprofit as "the solution."

Engaged. Are you working to build relationships with key media members and influencers? If you're just sending the occasional news release or announcement, you're not truly engaging with the people who are most likely to help your nonprofit tell its story.

Appealing Are the ideas you share with the media lively, current, relevant, and sexy? Do you have a good story to tell? Journalists often complain that nonprofit communications tend to be boring and announcements rarely change year after year. Make sure you're providing compelling information that will get the attention of a journalist—and resonate with your intended audiences.

Targeted. Many nonprofits use the "spray and pray" technique—pitching their story everywhere and praying that somebody picks it up. If your organization truly wants meaningful media coverage, avoid "spray and pray" and be surgical in your approach.

By following this framework, you'll improve your organization's chances to getting more regular—and higher value—media coverage. And you'll ultimately get more bang for your media relations' buck.

PART 2

G. is Goal Oriented

CHAPTER 6

What's Your Game Plan?

Setting Goals

Here's what passes for media relations strategy at a lot of nonprofits: when they're planning an event or announcing a new initiative, they create a news release, send it to every outlet in town, and hope someone picks it up.

When they inevitably fail to get much attention for the release, they complain that nobody covered their announcement and decide that they shouldn't invest much time and effort into pursuing media coverage.

In this case, however, the problem isn't the media. It's the nonprofit.

But there's a better way. To be successful with your media relations efforts, you don't necessarily need to invest a ton of time and money. But you need to be smart about how you allocate those resources. And it begins with having the right strategy.

Here are a few simple steps you can take to begin to build your strategy that will help your organization be more strategic with its media outreach.

Step One: Identify Your Organization's Goals

Effective media relations begin with understanding what your organization is actually looking to accomplish.

As a result, it's important that you not only have a strong understanding of your nonprofit's mission, but also have key strategic priorities to support that mission.

For the purposes of illustration, let's assume you work for a charity endeavoring to reduce the rate of childhood hunger. You might approach that mission through three key activities:

- Working with local and state governments to ensure there is adequate funding to support school-lunch and after-school food programs.
- Partnering with local companies to raise money and to collect food.
- Attracting volunteers who teach vulnerable families how to prepare healthy meals.

As the media manager, or the person responsible for communications in your organization, you will likely want to create a series of goals that correlate with these key activities. To do so, you might also talk to your organization's leadership and key staff to identify their priorities and ensure that your goals align.

As your organization's PR, media and/or communications pro—whether you are new in your position or you are looking to breathe new life into your organization's media relations efforts—begin the process with interviewing key members of your organization and take the time to identify key goals. Once you've identified them, put them front and center and make sure everything else you do supports these *goals*.

Step 2: Define Your Key Audiences

Many nonprofits make the mistake of thinking they need to reach *everybody* to be successful. But attempting to develop campaigns that reach the general population often leads to watered-down messages that fail to inspire *anyone* to take meaningful action.

A more successful approach is to identify two or three key audiences that you need in order to achieve each of your organization's goals.

In the example of our hunger charity above, it needs the support of some key audiences to achieve each of the articulated goals. For instance, to get local and state government to expand funding, you might start to target lawmakers and their staff as a key audience.

After you've identified who those audiences are, take some additional time to find out what makes those people tick. What motivates them? What do they enjoy? How do they want to be perceived? Some organizations develop personas for their target audiences. Personas are profiles of a fictional person who represents the qualities of the people in a target audience and are used to inform your organization of the target audience.

Regardless of whether you take the time to develop formal personas, it's important to know who you want to reach and to build all of your media plans around attracting those people.

Step 3: Identify Your Media Targets

It's only after you know who you want to reach and what you want to say to them that you can properly identify which media outlets are most important to your organization.

Again, your goal isn't to build relationships with every media outlet or to blast every outlet on your list each time you're looking to pitch a story. Instead, you're looking to build meaningful relationships with journalists at outlets that are most likely to reach your target audiences and talk about topics that align with your key messages.

You can start the process by analyzing the media outlets on your existing press list and assessing which of them are most likely to connect with your key audiences. You should also extend your search to include websites and networks that can help you reach these targets.

We recommend developing a list of high priority outlets for each audience you want to reach and each goal you're looking to achieve, and spending time researching what types of stories they cover. This will help you identify stories and angles that can guide your future pitches.

After spending a decade in corporate and nonprofit communications, Cindy Olnick, director of communications for the Los Angeles Conservancy, finally accepted the fact that there is no such thing as "The General Public." At one point her agency—which focuses on preserving historic buildings—was only getting press coverage during urgent situations, such as when an important building was threatened with demolitions. But since these opportunities were few and far between, Olnick began looking for other options. That's when she discovered a popular public radio podcast based on design and architecture that reaches their target demographic.

After that discovery, Olnick began speaking regularly with the podcast's hosts—with great results.

"Because we've helped them on so many stories, they listen to us when we pitch," Olnick said. "They care about what we do. It requires extra work, but it's worth it."

Developing and Implementing Your Strategy

Once you know your goals and have identified your audiences, it's time to start figuring out what you actually want to say.

To do this, take some time to identify key messages that will help motivate your target audiences to help your organization make progress on your goals.

If, for instance, you are looking to get elected officials in your state to put more money in the budget for school lunch programs, identify messages that are likely to get them to pay attention and to take action. You might even tailor those messages differently for Republican officials and Democratic officials.

These key messages will become central touch points to all of your communications and all of the stories you pitch to the media. Every story you pitch will seek to convey and to reinforce one or more of your organization's key messages.

If it doesn't reinforce one of those messages and move you closer to your goal, it's probably not worth pitching.

Involving Your Entire Team

Although many organizations don't have a full-time communications staff, it's still important to create a goal oriented team of individuals who can interact with the media. This team can also help hone and focus the messages and themes your group presents through the media to your members, volunteers, donors, supporters, friends, and stakeholders.

The team will likely include others outside of your organization's communications staff, and can help with creating story ideas that might appeal to different media organizations and proactively suggesting story ideas. No matter how many people you have on your team, certain bases need to be covered.

Work within your staff to develop ideas, but also to educate members, volunteers, and the board about finding and passing along information that could be the basis of a good news story for your group.

When sitting down with your team, determine who will handle the following responsibilities:

Writing

Determine who will create the "underpinning" for your media communications. This person will be responsible for consistent messages and themes across all media, as well as through your website, social media, press-kits and online press room.

Your organizational goals should provide the framework for your writer's efforts. This person should also create concise talking points so your spokesperson can "stay on message."

Note: There should not be a single communication that goes out from your organization that hasn't been read and edited by at least one person other than the writer.

Coordinating

Every effective team has an adept coordinator—someone who can manage and oversee tasks such as scheduling interviews, updating the organization's media lists and planning press luncheons. This responsibility should include cultivating and maintaining relationships with media personnel at all levels and working actively as a "media liaison" behind the scenes during special events or news conferences.

If you do not have a designated communications professional or PR person on staff, you might consider working with an agency to supply information to the media, respond to interview requests, and plan and coordinate photo opportunities.

Being the Spokesperson

Your organization should have one or more spokespeople who are articulate and at ease in front of a camera or microphone. But good spokespeople should be more than just good on camera. Make sure they are also:

- Have a clear understanding of your organization's media relations goals
- Well-informed about your group's issues, activities, events, and goals
- Able to think quickly and recognize trick or controversial questions
- Credible and able to develop a good rapport with those in the media
- Of good judgment, and able to exercise restraint when needed

- Intuitive enough to know when a reporter has an ax to grind with your cause or agency; and
- Adept enough to know how to counteract this ax-grinding without looking defensive or shifty.

Your spokespeople also need to be well prepared.

Ebony Hillsman, former media coordinator for Turner Broadcast Network and CNN, stressed the importance of having everyone on the same page. "So many times the PR staff would schedule interviews with the big names in the agency but when they sat down with us they had no idea what they were talking about." This was a major problem for live television or radio and resulted in producers calling on nonprofits with "subjects" they could trust. "People thought we had our favorites, and we did, based on who could deliver." We will talk more about preparing for interviews in Chapter Ten.

CHAPTER 7

Pitching with Purpose

Pitching has become a popular topic in the nonprofit world, but consider it from a baseball perspective. If you are the pitcher and you want to strike out a batter, you need to call the right pitches and spot them in the right places. This requires a certain amount of strategy. So let's consider your warm-up, step-up, and delivery.

Before you step up to the mound, consider what type of pitch you need to throw their way.

The Warm-up

In baseball, pitchers spend hours preparing to make deliveries that last a split second. The same level of preparation is needed for media relations pros who are pitching a story—whether and they're engaging a reporter in a phone, email or social media exchange.

In this case, your warm-up is research. For your pitch to hit the mark, it's important to make sure you follow our earlier recommendations about getting to know the reporters you most want to connect with before you even toe the rubber.

"The cold hard truth is that most people who work in media are drowning in a tsunami of email, research, and hard deadlines," says Claire Meyerhoff, president of The Planned Giving Agency, LLC, and former Washington-based broadcast journalist for CNN, CBS Radio, and SiriusXM.

As a nonprofit representative, it is perfectly legitimate to believe that your story is important and has value—because it does. But getting the media to recognize that value requires a game plan that begins with a great pitch. Media folks are strapped for time—and not because they are so popular or fabulous or busy having tons of awesome authentic human connections all the time. Rather, it's because of the sheer demand of production that involves editors, producers, sources, and the new equation of the 24-hour news cycle connected social media culture we live in. To strengthen your chances of pitching, put in some prep work."

The Set-up

According to Claire, before you call a reporter, you need to have a few things clear in your mind before beginning your pitch:

1. Have a hook. Why should your story be covered now? The Oregonian newspaper has one of the most helpful definitions of what news is. While hosting a fundraising event is probably considered news, you should still work on the elements in this list to make your event stand out. The larger your target media market, the harder you'll need to work to make your event sound special.

2. Ask yourself: why should this particular reporter care? Sometimes you end up calling a general assignment reporter, and that's fine. You can go with a more straight-forward

pitch. But if you want your story in the Business Section, you need to pitch a business reporter, and therefore your story should have a clear business angle. Stories about fund-raising could appear in virtually any section of the paper with the right angle and press release content. (Include quotes from elected officials, for example, if you're trying for the local section or talking to the government beat reporter, or quotes from business leaders if you're trying for the Business Section). If the reporter has previously written about your topic or organization, definitely mention that (for example: "You wrote a great story about this in May, and I think this would be an excellent follow-up.")

3. What can you offer besides the press release? Will there be good photo opportunities? Can you put the reporter in touch with several people to interview, people who donated to your silent auction, people who will benefit from the work that the fundraiser will help pay for—whoever can provide quotes that will support the story angle? Can you offer behind-the-scenes tours of particularly cool venues or backstage interviews with well-known keynote speakers or high-profile guests?

The Delivery

In baseball, once the ball leaves the pitcher's hand, the ultimate outcome depends on the hitter. You could deliver a perfect fastball on the outside corner of the plate and still not get the result you want.

The same is true with making a media pitch. Your ultimate success depends on the reporter. And sometimes, you can deliver a perfect pitch and the reporter simply won't swing. But if you follow Claire's three tips, you're more likely to throw something a reporter's way that can land your agency a home run in the media.

PART 3

R. is Responsive

CHAPTER 8

Being Accessible, Available, and Accurate

The explosion in digital and social media offers nonprofits a number of advantages. It gives organizations the opportunity to publish their own news through their websites, engage with reporters on social media, and establish their reputations as thought leaders.

But despite these advantages, today's media landscape is tough to navigate—especially for nonprofits with limited staff and resources.

It wasn't long ago that local nonprofits only had to worry about what was published in the local daily, on 3-4 TV stations, and on 1-2 local radio news stations.

Today, they need to pay attention to these outlets, plus a number of blogs and online news sites, social media accounts, podcasts, and online video. And they need to be able to respond and react quickly.

In this environment, it's easy for even the most sophisticated nonprofit to miss out on an important opportunity or get buried under an avalanche of negative comments.

Luckily, there are some shortcuts that can help you not only keep up with what's happening, but also to take advantage of the fast-moving nature of today's news. We recommend having structures and approaches in place that prepare you to play defense (reacting quickly to news situations that directly affect your nonprofit) and play offense (taking advantage of news events that are happening outside of your organization).

Playing Defense:
Build a Rapid-Response Protocol

In a today's media world, speed is critical.

You need more than a strong message—you need to be able to deploy this message to the right people at the right time.

If you move too slowly, you will miss opportunities to gain attention and change minds.

And if your organization is at the center of a controversy, the inability to respond quickly can have disastrous consequences.

Slow-footed nonprofits can lose donors, partners and grants if they cannot communicate effectively during a time of crisis. But nonprofits can take advantage of breaking-news opportunities and respond promptly to crises if they plan ahead.

One way to do this is to create a rapid response protocol.

A rapid response protocol will give your organization the process and the tools it needs to take advantage of breaking news opportunities or respond to an unexpected crisis.

If done well, your protocol will also include some pre-written talking points and key messages that you can grab and use during fast-moving news events.

We ask five key questions when we work with nonprofits and foundations to develop rapid response protocols. We've offered guidance on how to answer some of these questions in earlier sections of this book, but it's important to think about these questions in the context of rapid response.

1. Who are your designated spokespeople?

When news breaks, you need to have the right people prepared to speak on your behalf. Figure out who those people are ahead of time—rather than when the bullets are flying.

Some organizations choose one person as a key spokesperson. Others have a trusted group that might include the executive director, board members, the head of communications or other key leaders.

No matter your approach, make sure you know that you can reach at least one of your spokespeople on short notice and that they are well equipped to speak about your organization and its work.

2. Which issues do we care about most?

If your organization is looking to take advantage of events in the news, it's important to spend some time discussing the types of issues you care most about. By doing this, you'll be able to create filters and alerts that will help you identify opportunities quickly.

It will also help you develop draft pitches ahead of time that you can customize and deploy on the fly.

What are your key messages?

Your rapid response protocol should include a handful of key messages that connect with the issues your organization cares about, and that convey your values and mission.

These messages become the raw materials for written statements and social media postings, and can serve as a guide for your spokespeople if they're speaking to reporters.

And, by working through them ahead of time, you can cut down on the amount of time that's needed to get approvals for news releases and written statements.

3. Who are your highest priority media targets?

You don't want to waste time deciding which media members and outlets need to be contacted. Develop a shortlist of your highest-valued media members and spend time cultivating relationships with these reporters and editors.

These relationships will be incredibly valuable when events are moving quickly.

4. What is your process for releasing information?

Who has to sign off on written statements, news releases and social media postings? Is there a way to ensure that you can get these approvals quickly during crises or breaking news opportunities?

It's important to talk through this process ahead of time to make sure you're not stuck later. If you need to wait on a volunteer board chair to approve a statement, for example, you might get stuck if they are away for business or have their phone turned off at their daughter's dance recital.

Work through what happens if a key decision maker is unavailable. You might need to give multiple people the authority to approve what's released publicly, or to flatten your process to ensure that there are no hold ups.

5. What resources do we need?

Some organizations do not have the resources in house to respond quickly to breaking news.

If this is the case, you might need to have a consultant or agency who you can enlist to work on your behalf. It's important to identify that resource ahead of time rather than scrambling to find someone during a crisis.

Once you've answered these questions, it's important to put your protocol in writing and ensure that it is in the hands of the right people.

Some organizations identify a rapid response team that can deploy during breaking news events. Each member of this team should have a copy of the protocol, as well as a list of email addresses and cell phone numbers for people they need to connect with quickly.

Finally, it's important to make sure your protocol is reviewed regularly to ensure that your key messages are up-to-date, your spokespeople are prepared, and your media list is up-to-date.

Case study: When Breaking News Intersects With Mission

When National Football League star Adrian Peterson faced charges of child abuse in 2014, his case made national headlines.

It also thrust ESCAPE Family Resource Center in Houston and its CEO, Lidya K Osadchey, into the spotlight as an expert voice on the topic of child abuse and parental boundaries.

"Sometimes it's bad news when the media reaches out to us," says Osadchey, who works to prevent child abuse and neglect by providing education, intervention and support programs to families in crisis. "His indictment in the child abuse case opened conversations about how children are raised. This gave us an opportunity to raise awareness about all the research on the links between spanking and not understanding the developmental needs of children, leading to health issues and antisocial behavior. These are difficult and personal issues, but when a conflict shows up in a community, the media looks to us."

While many nonprofits have missions that focus on preventing child abuse, ESCAPE had already invested significant time and money in developing research and establishing its voice as a thought leader on the topic.

In addition, the organization made sure it was prepared for the situation by developing protocols that allowed it to respond quickly.

The takeaway?

By planning ahead and being responsive, nonprofits can stand out from the pack when media are looking for sources during fast-moving stories.

Playing Offense: Newsjacking

Amazon founder Jeff Bezos set the nonprofit world ablaze in the summer of 2017 when he tweeted a "request for ideas" about how to direct his charitable giving. Not surprisingly, Bezos' unusual public request has drawn massive media coverage, in addition to more than 42,000 replies on Twitter.

This is a perfect example of 'newsjacking' — the public relations practice of using a hot item in the news to help generate media coverage for your organization.

If employed well, newsjacking can be a highly successful tactic for nonprofits that are looking to draw attention to their cause or point of view. In the case of Bezos' plea for ideas, many nonprofits and foundations used his call as an opportunity to comment on their work in news stories, draft letters to the editor, and write pieces that appeared on social media.

When news breaks, reporters are often looking for fresh, thoughtful voices to put the news in context. And opinion pages are often looking for writers to respond to or add opinions about timely topics.

If you pay attention to the headlines with a critical eye, you will likely spot newsjacking opportunities for your nonprofit almost weekly.

For most nonprofits, news about government budgets and policy can have implications for their causes and the people they serve. If you are a nonprofit that specializes in health care, for example, the current push to repeal Obamacare is a prime newsjacking opportunity.

Newsjacking can also happen around stories about prominent figures coming to town to give a speech to local business groups.

If you're creative, you can even newsjack holidays. Many groups that work on LGBTQIA+ issues, for instance, have used Pride month as a newsjacking opportunity—leveraging the calendar to gain attention for their issues.

If your organization is looking to move beyond sending announce-ments about its own work—or if your goal is to position your nonprofit as a thought leader, advocate for its mission, or raise aware-ness about a key issue—you should consider embracing the tactic.

But before you dive in, it's important to note that newsjacking works best when it's done deliberately. You can't just wait for news to happen and expect to be able to tag along unless you do some work up front.

Here are six things to remember if you're looking to become a successful 'newsjacker':

1. Prepare your key messages up front

   Before you begin scouring Twitter or your local newspaper for newsjacking opportunities, you have to first know what you want to talk about when opportunities arise. Take time to have a clear sense of your larger communications goals and the key messages you want to express. Without taking this step up front, you're going to be scrambling when opportuni-ties do arise—and you'll actually struggle to identify the right newsjacking opportunities. However, if you know your key messages and have prepared your leadership to talk about those messages, you will be able to act quickly and know what you're talking about. This will give you an important leg up when it's time to act—and you'll be confident that you're saying the right things if a reporter does show up with a microphone or notebook in hand.

2. Develop relationships

   To newsjack effectively, it helps to know how to get to the right reporter or editor quickly. Sending pitches to general email boxes or calling a main newsroom line isn't likely to get you results. Instead, identify some outlets that are of high value to your organization, pay attention to who is getting bylines around the topics you care about, and start to build relationships with them. You can even tee up the fact that your organization has expertise in certain topics so that they know to come to you if they're searching for sources online. You don't need to rely just on phone calls or emails to begin to build these relationships. You can also start to follow journalists on Twitter and other social networks and start conversations informally.

3. Create protocols

   News moves quickly, and newsjacking requires an ability to make your pitch while a story is still hot. As a result, it's important to prepare your organization to make fast decisions. If you have to go through multiple layers of approval before you can send a news release or call a reporter, you're likely to lose opportunities. To overcome this hurdle, develop a rapid response protocol so that you can get your messages out when they matter, and that you can have your key spokespeople ready to go.

4. Pay attention

   To jack the news, you have to know the news. This means following key news outlets regularly—as well as paying attention to social media—to see what news is breaking. You can employ a number of tools to help: Google alerts around important keywords, lists of key Twitter accounts, etc.

5. Act quickly

   Newsjacking is most effective when you make your pitch

shortly after the news first breaks, and before the 'second-day' reports come out offering context.

6. Speak sensitively

   Newsjacking can backfire if you don't employ it with tact and sensitivity. The internet is littered with examples of companies and nonprofits that have tried to attach themselves to tragedies or disasters and have come across as tone deaf or opportunistic. Make sure you're acting tastefully and that your effort to draw attention is something that you and your organization will be proud of later.

By planning ahead—and developing a system to identify and react to opportunities quickly—your nonprofit can be able to spring into action the next time there's an opportunity to jack the news.

CHAPTER 9

Making Your
Event Media Friendly

It's impossible to discuss media relations for nonprofits without putting a special emphasis on events. Nonprofits spend countless hours—and considerable amounts of money—staging gala dinners, peer-to-peer fundraising campaigns, and other events that aim to draw attention to their work and rally their supporters to donate to their organizations.

Quite often, they also expect these events to generate media coverage, and they are often disappointed when the event is ignored by newspapers, TV stations, and online outlets.

During our work as journalists, we received countless pitches from charities, small and large, inviting us to cover their events. In almost every case, the pitches were earnest, and the causes seemed worthy. But in almost every case, we had to say no.

While the events were big deals to the organizations that were staging them, most of them simply didn't have a juicy enough angle for us to feel confident that we would walk away with a story that was strong enough to make the pages of either of our publications.

To get reporters' attention, your event needs to provide journalists with enough of a news hook to justify taking time away from pursuing other stories to be there. They need to be assured that if they choose to attend, they will come away with a strong story. If you are simply sending a news release announcing your event, do not be disappointed when those pitches are ignored.

The good news is that reporters actually like to cover charity events that come with a ready-made news hook. The stories themselves are easy to report, and they provide an opportunity to report on some "good news." But with so many charity events on the calendar, you need to take the time to sell them on why yours will help them tell an interesting and newsworthy story.

Here are five approaches that are likely to help you find success in getting the Media to your next event.

1. Provide Support to Debunk a Trend

One way to get the media to cover your event is to position it in the context of a larger trend—preferably a trend that hasn't been covered by the news outlet you're pitching.

Best Buddies Pennsylvania's annual fundraising walk in 2016 earned a feature in the *Pittsburgh Tribune-Review*, not because the paper routinely covers charity walks, but because the growth of the Best Buddies' event mirrored a larger trend in peer-to-peer fundraising—it was among a growing number of smaller, less-established events that had been showing success locally.

Smart communicators will often talk to the people who are planning the event to learn more about what's happening in the broader field, and they research other events and trends to see if they can find connections.

By taking this step—and then showing reporters how your event will help them write an interesting trend story—you have a better chance of getting them to pay attention.

2. Connect to a Current News Topic

Is your environmental nonprofit hosting its annual dinner on the eve of a major climate change summit? Is your soup kitchen hosting a fundraising event at the same time that Congress is considering changes to the way food stamps are administered?

One way to get the media interested in your event is to find a connection between its mission and something that's happening in the news. This provides reporters with a ready-made hook and questions to ask your leadership and attendees, and it gives you the extra benefit of helping raise awareness about an issue that connects closely with your work.

During an annual gathering of charity leaders in Erie, Pennsylvania, Peter ran into an old reporter friend who had decided to cover the event because it gave him the opportunity to talk to nonprofit leaders whose organizations were affected by a delay in approving Pennsylvania's state budget.

The reporter decided to cover the event because he knew he would have a chance to talk directly to attendees in between sessions. The event helped him get a diverse array of opinions and put a local face on a statewide story.

3. Provide Insider Access to a Speaker or Award

If your event is bringing in an outside speaker or guest, attempt to make arrangements with that person to be available for interviews with select media members—and find out what topics they are willing (or unwilling) to discuss. Often, you can arrange some time—either before the event begins or after the speech—for short interviews.

Not only will this help you get coverage for your event, it could help bolster your relationship with the reporters who are offered the opportunity to interview your speaker. The reporter might be more likely to pick up the phone and call you in the future for comment on a story—and to reply to your next pitch.

4. Find a Human Interest Story

We mentioned this in a previous chapter but this is worth repeating. Chances are, your fundraising walk or ride isn't going to get the attention of a reporter on its own. After all, your community likely holds multiple fundraising events every weekend.

But you know what does appeal to reporters? Stories of perseverance, overcoming obstacles, and people doing extraordinary things in the face of adversity.

Many nonprofit events involve people who have amazing stories and are supporting an organization because of a deep personal connection to the cause. Rather than simply putting out announcements about your event, take the time to find out more about the people who are participating and make them the center of your pitch. Your fundraising team likely knows these stories already and would love to help you shine the spotlight on an amazing volunteer or a supporter who is walking in honor of a family member.

It takes a bit of extra work to find these stories and position them to reporters, but your chances of success are much higher if you can find a compelling person to be the face of your event.

5. Invite a Preview

Because many nonprofit-led events occur on nights and weekends—at times when most news organizations run with a skeleton crew—getting a reporter to actually come out to those events can be a stretch. But you don't need a reporter to come to the actual event to claim victory with your pitch. Often, you can gain more value by getting coverage ahead of the event. In addition to inviting reporters to attend your event, give them the option of writing a preview, and use one of the other tactics outlined above to help provide the hook.

6. Don't Forget That the Media is Attending

After putting all the effort into event planning, people often forget about the media that does plan to attend. Like all the aspects of event planning, creating a media-friendly event checklist will help you get the best stories from the media that attends. And trust us, if you treat reporters well, they will remember, and they might even rally editors to cover future events.

Media-Friendly Event Checklist

Before the event, refer reporters to the following:

- An up-to-date online newsroom. Press releases should include the most recent details and changes. Include high-resolution images, videos, or photos. (See Chapter Four for more on online newsrooms.)
- Event-specific page on your website to "join the conversation" with links to social media sites. (Encourage journalists to follow you before the event so you can follow back and they don't have to spend time looking for you during the event.)

- Send the media an invitation to the designated area. Provide them with an easily identifiable press pass so that they can gain access to capture event images. This will also alert guests and volunteers that they are talking to the press. Ideally, try to have a private room or location where they can have a quiet place to write and comfortably interview sources or spokespeople. Having quality internet access is essential. Set up work/charging stations. If you have passwords, be sure to post those at this location.
- Make sure the VIPs stop by. If your executive officer is going to be busy at the event, have an established spokesperson. In this situation, the leadership should have plenty of time to prepare, and it helps to have more than one designee.
- Have a volunteer staff the media room. It's important to have a physical body in place for logistical questions. Many of the media will assume they need to find the executive officer, but the volunteer should also have alternate numbers for the designees.
- After the event, follow-up with with a word of thanks and offer to provide any additional information

Media Hosting Do's and Don'ts

Do	Don't
Offer a free ticket for paid events with a press pass	Try to bribe the reporter with gifts
Make sure members of the media are clearly labeled so others know who they are talking to at the event	Let them roam around without directing them to some well-informed sources

Try to keep the messy aspects of the event/event drama away from the reporter	Make the mistake of thinking anything they see or hear is off the record
Ask if you can email them quotes, stats, etc. after the event	Expect them to let you see the story before it airs or is printed
Ask for corrections if they make a factual error	Be brash about asking for corrections (or that could be your last piece of coverage)

CHAPTER 10

Coaching Your Team
for Interviews

When preparing a member of your nonprofit's team for interviews or meetings with the media, you invariably spend time coaching them on what to say and how to act when the camera is rolling or when the reporter is scribbling notes.

But do you also prep them for what to do when the "on air" light is off or when the reporter closes the notebook? If you aren't, you're overlooking a crucial detail—one that can lead to some unfortunate headlines.

That's because everything that happens during that encounter—from the moment you say hello to the moment you're out of sight—is considered on the record. In other words, every statement you make can end up being reported.

To be sure, there are times when you can mutually agree to go off the record and we'll get into the mechanics of going off the record shortly. But unless you deliberately take that step, you should keep in mind that you're "on".

As a result, if you're preparing a member of your nonprofit's team for an appearance or interview, it's important that you take the time to let that person know what that means.

Unfortunately, a seemingly private comment about a cranky board member or an off-color joke is fair game—and it could end up working its way into a story.

Claiming after the fact that you didn't know that the statement made off camera, or after the formal interview, could be included doesn't cut it. By law—and by practice—journalists assume that you know the rules and they are often looking for well-schooled sources to say something candid or off the cuff.

This shouldn't scare you away from doing interviews. It just means you need to act and speak deliberately.

Here is some advice on how you should prepare for some common situations.

Interviews With Print Media Journalists

When working as a writer for newspapers and magazines, Antionette often unearthed some great information after closing her notebook at the end of a formal interview.

Often, as she and a source would exchange informal chit chat and discuss next steps, the source—feeling more relaxed—would offer some interesting perspectives or anecdotes that added to the story being pursued or provided an idea for another piece.

Her practice would typically be to say "I'd like to use that, do you mind if I follow up or ask you more about it now?"

Almost always, the source would agree to share more information.

But even if the source didn't want to share more, there wasn't much they could do about what they had already said—other than refuse to take additional questions about it or attempt to steer the conversation in another direction.

When meeting with a print reporter—a term that, for the sake of this book, includes those who write articles for newspapers, magazines or the web—there is typically a period of time before and after the formal interview where you exchange greetings and goodbyes.

Make sure you reinforce this point with your organization's representative ahead of the interview—and let that person know that the entire conversation is on the record. If the representative has concerns, offer some potential topics of conversation that they can bring up during these more informal portions of the interview—and discuss some things they should avoid saying or doing.

Interviews with Radio, Television & Broadcast Media

Recent history is littered with examples of politicians and celebrities who have gotten themselves in hot water for saying something that was picked up by a 'hot mic'.

President Donald Trump, one assumes, likely wishes he had kept his mouth shut when he was engaging in "locker room talk" with Billy Bush on that Access Hollywood tour bus. Same goes for Robert Durst, who was caught on microphone talking to himself about his role in a high-profile series of murders during the taping of a documentary series.

The lesson for nonprofit communicators is simple—if you're going on television or on the radio, assume that everything you say is getting picked up on a microphone, even if you're not technically "on air".

Even if the camera does not appear to be rolling or the radio segment has gone to commercial, you should assume the audio is being recorded and that anything you say can be picked up and used later.

Again, it's important to emphasize this point to representatives from your organization who are not experienced with on-air interviews to be sure that they are aware of the ground rules and are well prepared.

There are a number of reasons why nonprofit communications professionals shouldn't be lone rangers when it comes to media relations.

Here are a few tips for those struggling to get buy-in from your entire team:

Make it easy. Have a shared file that provides basic information. For special events consider creating an internal memo or a media relations handout with basic talking points, cell phone numbers, or a guide on how to find the spokespersons.

Reward and celebrate great stories in the office. Consider gathering clips of great newspaper stories that highlight the staff person involved. Put them in a common space or the staff person's office. It might sound cheesy, but you will be surprised about how many people respond to visible praise.

Continue training yourself and others. The media climate will continue to change, and auditing and updating strategies is a continuous process. Stay in-tune with media relations and communications-related blogs like Nonprofit Marketing Guide (www.nonprofitmarketingguide.com/blog) or On Message (https://www.turn-two.co/blog/). We also encourage you to gift this book; share sections or chapters; and encourage your teammates to join webinars, read related blog posts, and discuss.

CHAPTER 11

Responding in a Crisis

Nonprofits do important work that aims to make the world a better place.

Nevertheless, nonprofits are not immune to crises. Big-name organizations such as the Wounded Warrior Project, American Red Cross, Planned Parenthood, Susan G. Komen for the Cure, and others, have all found themselves in the media's (and public's) crosshairs in recent years. The same holds true for a number of smaller nonprofits.

Media crises involving nonprofits come in a number of forms. They can involve questions about improper spending, excessive salaries, unfortunate statements, or controversial stances. They can also happen to organizations of any size and with any mission.

Even if your organization does everything by the book, you should make sure you have a crisis communications protocol just in case something goes awry.

"How you prepare for a potential crisis and how you react to it are vital in the first stages of a crisis," according to Christina Adeleke,

Esq., communications and development coordinator from the North Carolina AIDS Action Network. "The main thing is to work on your crisis plan and skills before a crisis hits."

Here's some advice on what you can do to ensure that you're ready to respond appropriately and ethically to a crisis:

Creating a Crisis Team

Your organization should have a designated crisis team that you can mobilize quickly, if needed. Typically, this group will include your CEO or executive director, your head of communications, and your board chair. Some organizations choose to include other top executives and/or their legal counsel as part of this team. This group should be considered always on call and empowered to make rapid decisions about how to handle a crisis.

Because crises don't always happen between 9:00 a.m. and 5:00 p.m. on weekdays, contact information for this group should be at the fingertips of your communications director or top executive—and members of this team should be informed in advance that they could receive a midnight phone call if needed.

With any luck, that midnight call will never happen, but it's important to make sure you're ready in case it does.

Designate a Spokesperson

If your organization is facing a crisis, you should designate someone who is empowered to speak on your behalf. This person will often be your top executive. In some cases, though, you might choose to have your communications directors or board chair fill this role.

This person should be prepared to face tough questions and be briefed on the facts before taking questions. Whoever fills this role should have some experience in front of the camera—and you might consider providing them with media training so that they are equipped to handle the heat.

When Should You Issue a Statement?

Silence is your worst enemy in a crisis. The longer you wait to make a statement, the more it looks like you have something to hide. With the advent of social media, false information can travel quickly; therefore, you should put together a written statement that shares everything you know about the situation—consult an attorney or HR professional on how much detail to put in the statement. Tell the truth.

Crises often grow worse when organizations withhold information that—when revealed later—makes it look like they were hiding something. State the facts clearly and, in cases where you're investigating what happened, make it clear that you're still gathering information.

As you draft your statement, try to step outside your role with the organization and think about what you would want to know as an outsider who is reading or seeing a story about the situation. What would make you trust the organization? What would force you to doubt its accounts?

Be careful about jumping to conclusions in your statement. Sometimes, you simply need to share the basics and acknowledge that you're gathering the facts. If the story is fast moving, you cannot afford to wait until you have all of the information before you put out a statement. Get something out quickly, show that you're on top of it, and say that you'll have more to share later.

Coordinate with Others

In some cases, your organization's crisis might involve other groups such as law enforcement or another nonprofit. In these situations, identify the spokespeople for these organizations and, if possible, work to coordinate your efforts.

Have a Media Kit Prepared

In crises, it's also necessary to provide context. Your organization does great work and has a mission—don't be afraid to make the media and public aware of what you do and why you do it.

At the very least, you should develop a fact sheet about your organization ahead of time that outlines what you do, your outcomes, and other vital information on how you operate (including facts about your budget and history). Make it as easy as possible for the media and your supporters to obtain context and information that helps people understand who you are and what you do.

Keep this information up-to-date and ready for whenever you're talking to a member of the media—whether it's for a positive story or a crisis.

Manage the Message

Whenever possible, try to direct the media to talk to your designated spokesperson, but also understand that reporters will be looking for multiple sources. If the story is big enough, a reporter might contact other members of your staff, members of your board, donors, volunteers, or others who are connected to your organization.

Be prepared for this by communicating clearly with your team, your board, and your supporters about the situation. Provide them with information about what you know, and offer them advice for handling questions.

Be Honest

It bears repeating that you should always aim to tell the truth. This is especially true in a crisis. Tell as complete a story as you can, and if you don't know the answer to something, don't speculate. Make it clear that you don't know the answer. If you learn relevant information—positive or negative—that affects the story, meet with your crisis team to discuss it and decide how to address it, whether it's by issuing an update or being prepared to talk about it when questioned.

Crises tend to disappear more quickly when you get in front of the story, acknowledge your mistakes, and show that you're moving forward.

With any luck, you may never have to follow this advice. However, if your organization ever faces a controversy, planning ahead and being upfront can help you deal with it quickly and responsibly.

When Should You Put Out a Statement?

Nonprofits should almost always issue a statement if they are the subject of a controversy. But organizations sometimes opt to release statements about events and issues that aren't directly related to the organization and its work.

When is it appropriate for your nonprofit to release a statement?

Here are some factors to consider to help you decide whether to issue a statement—or stay silent:

The connection to your mission. Your organization's leadership might have a strong opinion about controversial topics, such as the 2017 controversy over protests during the National Anthem at NFL games. But does taking a stand on these protests connect directly with your mission? If you're a military charity, work in civil rights, or work to defend the First Amendment, it might make sense to craft a statement that shares your organization's stance. But if you run a food bank, the connection isn't as clear—and you might be better off saving your power for another issue.

Will the right people care? Is the media likely to be calling your leadership for comment? Are your supporters likely to be curious about your stance on an issue? If the answer to either of these questions is yes, you might consider crafting and releasing a statement. If not, releasing a statement might take time away from addressing more pressing matters in your organization.

Do you have something meaningful to say? Avoid making a statement just for the sake of making a statement. If you don't have a strong viewpoint or a clear call to action, it's likely that your statement will lack impact or get ignored.

Will you gain or lose support? A statement about changes to immigration might help whip your existing supporters into action and raise your visibility with potential donors. But for some groups, such a statement might have the opposite effect—which could not only cost your organization revenue, but serve as a distraction from your work. It's important to assess the impact of your statement on supporters before you decide to make it. Ultimately, you might decide that the risk of losing support is worth it because your organization believes it is crucial to your mission. But it's important to make this assessment up front—and prepare for the potential consequences.

If, after reviewing these factors, your organization decides that it should make a public statement, you have more options than ever for making sure that statement is seen and heard.

Rather than drafting a full-blown news release, your organization can make a shorter, more focused statement that it can post on its website and on social media so it gains maximum exposure.

If you're hoping that it will get seen and picked up by the media, you can also email it directly to key reporters and news outlets.

But before you can send your statement far and wide, you'll have to write it.

Here are a few things to remember as you put it together:

Keep it short. You don't need to write a treatise when you're making a public statement about a timely topic. Often, a few sentences will express your organization's opinion and ensure that people can understand your point of view.

Keep it real. Avoid jargon and flowery words. Instead, craft it in a voice that is both direct and clear. If one of your goals is to get your statement quoted by the media, it stands a much better chance if it's clear, direct, and simple.

Be careful. If your statement is about a sensitive topic, make sure you have it reviewed by experts such as your legal counsel, or a key member of your board, to be sure that you're not courting trouble.

PART 4

E. is Empowered

CHAPTER 12

When the Media Gets It Wrong

There's an adage in public relations that there's no such thing as bad publicity. But while this might be true if you're a celebrity or a political candidate, bad publicity can have dire consequences for nonprofits.

When you manage the reputation of a nonprofit that is working to advance an important mission, incorrect information—particularly if it's reported in the media—can damage your ability to raise money and effectively advocate for change.

This is especially true in a digital media world, where errors can take on a much longer life than ever before. In the pre-internet days, most mistakes would disappear quickly from the public's consciousness—seen only by those who watched a live newscast or read a story in print.

But today's errors can have a lasting footprint. A news story about your organization can score high in online search rankings for years—meaning that every time someone searches your nonprofit's name on Google or on your local newspaper's website, they will be exposed to that mistake.

With that in mind, it's more important than ever to attempt to get mistakes corrected.

Unfortunately, most errors never get fixed—in large part because those who notice the errors never speak up. A 2009 piece in Nieman Reports estimates that only one in 10 news sources actually reach out to newspapers about errors they've identified. While that figure is now a bit dated, our own conversations with communications professionals suggest that it hasn't changed much. Many groups just assume their complaints won't be heard—so they stay silent.

However, as a nonprofit communications pro, you shouldn't be shy about reaching out to the media when they get something wrong. Even if it doesn't yield an immediate correction, reaching out to a reporter or editor can help plant a seed for future coverage of the issue.

So how should you approach news outlets that miss the mark?

Your approach should depend, in part, on the nature of the inaccuracy. Some errors are very clear (a misspelled name or an incorrect number). Others are more open to interpretation.

Here is a high-level guide to help you navigate some common situations involving inaccurate, or incomplete, reporting.

Factual Errors

Most journalists strive to get it right. While there are bad actors that masquerade as fair-minded reporters and editors, most of the journalists who I've worked with are genuinely concerned about accuracy and will agree to hear out a source that believes they got something wrong.

If you've found a factual error, reach out politely by phone or email and explain the error—and why it's wrong. If possible, provide documentation or factual materials to support your claim.

Make it clear that you want to help them ensure that their reporting is factual and that you don't want to see an error get repeated.

When presented with a clear error, reporters who care about their craft will make sure it gets corrected—via a written correction and by updating the version that appears online.

If the reporter is unwilling to correct something that is clearly an error, ask to speak with their editor.

Often, these situations are fairly straightforward and, if you approach them properly, you can use it to help position your organization in a positive light for future stories. If the reporter feels as though you are fair-minded and reasonable, they will be more likely to reach out in the future.

Errors of Omission

In a world where the greatest rewards come to those who can publish a story first, news organizations aren't always as thorough as they should be in making sure they have all of the facts—or have taken the time to get all of the important sides of a complex issue.

This has always been a problem in the news business. When time is short, reporters can't—or don't—always get the whole story. Sadly, this problem has only grown worse in the internet age.

As a result, it's not uncommon for nonprofits to find their perspectives missing from stories that touch their work. In these cases, it's important not to stay silent.

While reaching out to reporters to alert them that they missed something in a story might not yield a correction, it can bring other results. In a developing story online, it could lead to a new version that includes your organization's viewpoint. It could prompt the reporter to do a follow-up story. It might also give the reporter something to think about when they cover a similar topic in the future.

When you approach reporters to talk about something that was left out, make it clear that you're looking to provide a perspective that they might not have known about—or that their other sources didn't share. Make it clear that your organization is a resource to them—and be willing to discuss ways in which they can either add to their existing reporting on the topic or ensure that they are covering the issue from all sides in the future.

Such instances can also bring opportunities to provide your own written commentary—whether through an opinion piece or a letter to the editor.

One-Sided Attacks

Today's media climate also includes websites and other outlets that clearly espouse a partisan point of view or produce content through a particular slant.

Often, these outlets will produce pieces that twist information or leave out key facts at the expense of those who have different points of view. Unfortunately, you can't expect to get many of these outlets to correct a story—or give you equal time. Nor is it necessarily wise to attempt to post a comment or agree to an interview.

But since some of these sites have a large online presence, their influence cannot be ignored. Rather than stepping into the lion's den—and possibly getting your organization's viewpoint trampled or twisted—it's often best to use your own channels to tell your story and offer a counterpoint. While the internet and social media have made it easier than ever for errors to spread, they also make it easier for nonprofits to speak about their work and the issues they care about.

If the media is getting that story wrong, not only do you have an obligation to try to get that story corrected—you have an opportunity to set the record straight on your website and your social media channels.

Don't squander those channels. Use them. Post a piece on your blog. Create a posting on Facebook and encourage your supporters to share it. If necessary, write a letter or email to your supporters. In a world where every organization is a publisher, you have the power to set your own narrative by speaking directly to your supporters and urging them to serve as your voice.

When a crisis occurs we recommend that agencies act fast, but with the understanding that some matters require consultation with an attorney. In particular, issues related to:

Defamation/ Slander/Libel	Defamation is an area of law that provides a civil remedy when someone's words end up causing harm to your reputation or your livelihood. Libel is a written or published defamatory statement, while slander is defamation that is spoken.
Personnel/HR	Every organization has a need to keep certain information confidential. HR is typically entrusted with maintaining sensitive employee data and information relating to employee and management issues. As a result, confidentiality issues in any human resource department are complex and multi-tiered. Sharing reasons for dismissal, resignation, and even periods of extended leave, with the media could result in a legal issue for the agency.
Liability	In certain cases, accusations of nonprofits (including of staff, volunteers, and board members) can lead to questions regarding the liability of an organization. Remember to consult the board of directors as they are the legal, governing body of a nonprofit corporation. They collectively represent the organization and its interests and should be a part of the discussion of engaging an attorney.

When Should You Consult an Attorney?

Christina Adeleke, Esq., communications and development coordinator at the North Carolina AIDS Action Network, offers the following advice about when to consult with an attorney:

- Remember that things said in the midst of crisis communications are subject to legal scrutiny. "Lawsuits happen and how you act up until that point matters," Adeleke says. "You have to be very intentional not to make certain offers or admit guilt."

- "Draw a line between PR versus legal." The topics above are clear indicators that should spark a discussion about legal engagement. Communications and PR staff shouldn't hesitate to level up issues that seem to venture into the legal realm. "Asking if this is a legal issue is never a stupid question."

Handling 'Fake News'

One of the byproducts of the nasty 2016 Presidential Election is the explosion of so-called 'fake news'—false information that is presented as fact by websites that appear to be authored by journalists but are instead authored by those looking to deceive (or, in some cases, create satire).

Fake news isn't actually new. Phony sites and shoddy reporters have been pumping out false information for a long time—so much so that fact-checking sites like Snopes.com and FactCheck.org have been patrolling the internet for years to debunk fake information.

But fake news exploded in 2016 during the Presidential campaign, when phony stories with wild headlines about the two candidates dominated our Facebook feeds and led many internet users astray.

Since the election, a number of companies have also been caught up in controversies that were based on false information spread online. According to PR Week, Pepsi had to deal with a potential boycott from Trump supporters after fake news stories erroneously quoted its CEO saying that Trump supporters should "take their business elsewhere." The shoe company New Balance, meanwhile, faced its own controversy from anti-Trump supporters, after a fake quote attributed to an executive stated that New Balance is the "official brand of the Trump revolution."

In this context, it's easy to see how nonprofits can get caught up in the fake news trap. It wouldn't take much for a liberal-leaning charity to get caught in the crosshairs of a controversy drummed up by a conservative fake-news outlet—or for a left-leaning site to make up salacious stories about the leader of a religious charity.

What should you do if this happens to your organization?

Here are three strategies to follow:

1. Debunk it Quickly

It's important to put out a statement to your supporters and others that the story is fake. Provide as much information as you can, including details about the credibility of the news source and the author, and sharing any information you can about your organization that counters the claim.

Speed is important here. As Winston Churchill once said, "A lie gets halfway around the world before the truth has a chance to get its pants on." Get your pants on quickly—and don't be afraid to say that the fake news source's own pants are on fire for its lie.

2. Put Out Positive Messages

New Balance was able to contain some of the damage surrounding its fake news controversy by putting out a number of messages about what its brand stands for and its history. Don't be afraid to toot your own horn and let the world know what you stand for as much as possible.

3. Avoid the Trolls

In addition to acting quickly and putting out positive messages, it's important to avoid getting into a back and forth with internet and social-media commenters who are trying to make you look bad by insulting you and twisting your words. Your best bet in these situations is to ignore—and, if possible—to block them.

Doing Your Part

Finally, even if your organization isn't the victim of a fake news controversy, you can do your part in tamping down fake news by being careful about the information you share through your social networks and website.

While it might be tempting to quickly retweet something that might be damaging to an organization or person with different views, make sure that the information is credible before sharing it. If it comes from a site you don't recognize, check out the source to make sure it's legit before putting it out under your organization's brand.

What to Do When the Story is Wrong

Your organization has a number of options if it is the victim of an incorrect or slanted story. Below are some common options—along with how and when to ask for or employ them:

Corrections

You can ask a news outlet to issue a correction when it makes a factual error (or errors) in the course of reporting a story.

When requesting a correction, it's important to have as much factual information as possible to prove that an error was made. Most corrections are fairly cut and dried—and reputable news outlets will issue them promptly and make updates to any versions of the story that appear online.

It's important to note that most news outlets publish or air corrections in a standard place and format (such as on page 2 of a newspaper's "A" section or on the bottom of its editorial page) and that they typically won't re-run or re-air a piece that included a factual error.

Our philosophy is to ask for another story rather than corrections that are often buried in some obscure place in the paper or online.

Retractions

Retractions are less common—and are considered to be the result of much more serious or malicious errors—than corrections.

If you followed the story of disgraced reporter Stephen Glass (popularized in the movie *Shattered Glass*), you know that some falsehoods aren't the result of a mistaken or misunderstood fact. Some of them are the result of fabricated reporting (or in some cases, sources who deliberately present reporters with false information to influence their reporting).

News outlets will typically offer retractions when they have reported a story that is fundamentally wrong. In these rare cases, the story doesn't include an error or even a number of errors, but is based on a false premise or false information that is later proven to be incorrect.

Hopefully, your nonprofit is never involved in a story that reaches this level. But if it is ever the victim of a story that is based on lies or falsehoods, it's important to quickly and decisively register your complaint and provide evidence that the story is wrong.

If an outlet does retract a story, it will usually pull it down from all of its online accounts—including social media—and will publish or air a retraction that explains the falsehood, why it happened, and how it is responding.

A retraction is basically an admission of journalistic malpractice, so it's not something that outlets are quick to decide to do. So make sure you have ample reason to believe that the outlet has overstepped its bounds before you demand one.

But it's an important tool to have if you ever do need it.

Letters to the Editor

In the case of stories that get the facts right, but leave out a key point or tackle a controversial topic, your nonprofit might choose to submit a letter to the editor to raise issues or arguments that you don't feel are properly addressed in the story.

This allows you to make your point—and even take exception to a story.

For newspapers and magazines, letters to the editor are typically published in a stand-alone section and grouped together.

In many cases, you'll need to submit your letter to a specific editor who will review it and decide whether or not to publish it. Submitting a letter is no guarantee that it will get published. Often, outlets will receive dozens, if not hundreds, of letters each day and will only have space to publish a fraction of them.

What's more, they will often only publish a portion of the selected letters so that they can accommodate as many voices as possible.

Because of this, a submitted letter should be short, direct and to the point. Don't spend time writing 2-3 page letters. Instead, come up with 2-3 strong paragraphs that clearly articulate your viewpoint.

This is easier said than done, of course. Stating an argument in two paragraphs can often be more challenging than doing so in two pages.

Comments

While your nonprofit might face long odds in getting its letter to the editor approved for publication, it has another, more democratic, avenue for expressing its opinion: online comments.

Most media outlets provide a comments section that appears with stories that are published or aired online. And if your organization wants to register its opinion about a piece, it certainly has the option of posting a comment.

Online comments offer immediacy—as well as the opportunity to post your opinion without fear of having it cut down by a space-conscious editor.

But we advise you to tread carefully before you post a comment. On many news sites, comments sections can be infested with ruthless attackers and trolls. And while these comments can sometimes be entertaining, if you are posting a comment on a site that is known for bilge, you run the risk of not only opening your organization up to some nasty slings but of being seen as just another member of the peanut gallery rather than a serious organization doing serious things.

Having said that, there are some spaces where posting a comment has value.

One of Peter's clients, for instance, recently saw *The Economist* write a piece that left out its perspective on an issue. Knowing the

The Economist's comments section tends to be a bit more serious than, say, the *Washington Post's,* he worked with the client to craft a signed comment that articulated its viewpoint—with the idea that those who cared about the issue need to know that perspective to fully understand the issue.

CHAPTER 13

Becoming a Thought Leader

Like many small nonprofits, College Directions Inc. doesn't have a media relations team that can devote hours each week to courting news reporters or sending out news releases.

For years, the organization had tried—often in vain—to pitch stories to the media about its work and programs. But in 2015, it decided to try a new approach.

Instead of pitching the occasional press release to newspapers and TV stations, CDI would work to position itself as an expert voice on the challenges faced by low-income and first-generation college students—an expertise that aligns closely with its mission. To do that, it would develop written pieces that offered a point of view on the issue—and would seek opportunities to share those pieces in its existing network and in media outlets.

CDI was looking to position itself as a thought leader.

Thought leaders use their opinions and expertise to brand themselves as the go-to voices in their field, says Denise Brosseau, a thought-leadership consultant and the award-winning author of *Ready to Be a Thought Leader?: How to Increase Your Influence, Impact, and Success*. By doing so, they become trusted sources and are able to inspire people to follow them and take action.

Nonprofits have always used thought leadership as a way to gain attention for their work. Often, organizations would position charismatic leaders, researchers, and others as experts—relying on assets like speeches, newspaper opinion pieces, and research papers to showcase themselves as experts.

But, today, nonprofits have an even larger array of ways to demonstrate thought leadership and, in turn, gain attention for their expertise.

In addition to publishing research and submitting formal pieces to newspapers and magazines, nonprofits can now leverage their own channels—such as blogs, email newsletters, and social media accounts—to highlight their ideas, build a following, and gain attention. By sharing their ideas and opinions through these channels, nonprofits can sometimes gain media coverage and build relationships with journalists. Many reporters will follow nonprofits on social media and others will come across their written work and videos when they are researching stories on their own. If non-profit executives are able to position thoughtful commentary and opinions through these channels, they're far more likely to have reporters knocking on the door when they're looking for smart voices for their stories.

This doesn't happen by accident. Successful thought leaders are often quite deliberate in their approach—and they sometimes take months, if not years, honing their messages and building their reputations.

Practical Advice from an
Expert on Thought Leadership

If your organization is interested in becoming a thought leading organization, Brosseau suggests answering the following questions before you get started:

Who is the most likely person to represent your organization as a thought leader? Is it the CEO, communications director, a board member, or a combination of people? Are you selecting the person with the most knowledge on a subject or someone who truly wants to change the world within their area of passion? The latter is likely your best bet.

"Individuals with expertise, passion, and a track record of changing the world become thought leaders when they rise above themselves by sharing their knowledge so others can change the world, too," Brosseau says.

What topic does your nonprofit want to focus on? Often, your thought leadership is guided by your mission or those impacted by that mission. "Many thought leaders start as leaders of an initiative, program, company, or organization," Brosseau says. "In that role, they see the need for a change—a different future than would otherwise occur—not just in their workplace or community, but much more broadly. They feel a calling to bring about that change—often regardless of the odds and despite any setbacks and challenges.

Where does thought leadership begin? "Some people use the term 'thought leader' as if all you have to do to earn that moniker is to start tweeting. This is hardly the case," she says. "To bring about the future they envision, they may step into a broader role as a convener or participant in an advisory

committee, task force, industry consortium, or professional asso-
ciation. They may advocate for new legislation or modifications
to existing regulations that impact an industry as a whole—not
just [those] that benefit their own company. Others take to a
'bully pulpit' by writing op-eds, crafting white papers, and so on.
They argue for a fundamental rethinking of an entire process—
not just incremental change."

CDI answered all three of these questions before pursuing its
thought leadership strategy.

It chose its president, Rachel Pfeifer, as the voice of the
organization.

It selected issues that are unique to low-income and first-
generation college students as the topic they would focus on.

Guided by events in the news, CDI looked for opportunities
to inject its voice into broader conversations that were happening
in the media and in other venues around the issues facing college
students.

In February 2016, when the president of Mount St. Mary's
University in Baltimore made headlines for advocating to have
struggling freshmen leave their school in order to help boost their
retention rate, CDI knew they had found the perfect situation for
raising their voice with a different perspective.

With help from CDI's communications manager, Pfeifer penned
an op-ed piece that challenged the university President's stance.

The piece was quickly published by *The Baltimore Sun*. This
represented a huge win for CDI—injecting its president's voice into
a high-profile debate that was central to its mission.

But the victories didn't stop there. After seeing her essay in
the Baltimore Sun, editors at *The New York Times* invited Pfeifer

to contribute a piece to appear in its Room for Debate feature. In short order, this small charity was suddenly speaking to one of the largest audiences in the US.

"This has been a wonderful experience for CDI," says Juliana Avery, CDI's former communications manager. "We are happy to have made our voice heard on an important issue. It has energized our board and supporters, and it has raised the profile of the organization."

It also helped get results. Facing public pressure, the university's president resigned—and CDI helped lead a larger discussion about the issues surrounding low-income and first-generation college students.

Trista Harris, president of the Minnesota Council on Foundations, has taken a slightly different approach to burnishing her reputation as a thought leader. Earlier in her career, Harris began speaking and writing about how to improve diversity among nonprofit leaders. Later, she advocated for younger leaders to have a more powerful voice in their organizations. Today, that role has evolved into advocating for new leaders who work at nonprofits and foundations.

Along the way, she has been quoted in *The Chronicle of Philanthropy* and *The New York Times*, appeared on CNN, and been featured on numerous social sector blogs. Harris has also co-authored the book *How to Become a Nonprofit Rockstar*, and she now speaks internationally about using the tools of futurism in the social sector.

Harris said she was able to build her reputation, in part, by connecting with experts such as Brosseau and using low-cost resources that helped her learn how to present her opinions.

"I looked for free media training and watched YouTube videos on how to prepare for interviews, which is how I learned to be tweet-able and speak in digestible quotes," Harris says.

She also spent a few minutes each day scrolling through journalism matchmaking services (like the ones mentioned in Chapter Six) and encourages communications professionals to do the same.

Nonprofits should consider taking a number of other simple steps to help ensure success for their thought leadership programs.

Do you want to be responsive as a thought leader?

1. **Create an online presence.** Likely on your "About Us" page or in your online newsroom, provide bios of your organization's thought leaders, links to published interviews, and/or videos of their speeches and media appearances. This will provide reporters with evidence that your thought leaders are credible, well-spoken experts.

It's worth noting that comments you make on social media —whether through Twitter, Facebook, Instagram or another source—are all "on the record." Increasingly, media outlets are quoting statements made by individuals on these social networks in their reporting.

As a result, it's important for officials at your organization to recognize this fact and be careful both about what they post and what they comment on.

If you wouldn't want what you said on Facebook to appear in your local newspaper or on the TV news, it's probably best not to say it at all.

2. **Answer the call.** If you are serious about becoming a thought leader, make it your goal to return media inquiries promptly. We recommend responding to all media inquiries within 24 hours,

but it's likely that you will need to be available to do so even more promptly during breaking news events. Media members are likely to come back to you if they know that you're available and accessible.

3. **Know your stuff.** Before you begin branding yourself as a thought leader—and before each media inquiry—make sure you know your subject matter and that you're up-to-date on the latest news and trends related to your subject. Often this means not just knowing the appropriate facts and figures, but also having stories and anecdotes that can help illustrate your key points.

4. **Act proactively.** Keep your eyes open for opportunities to comment on current events and trends. If your organization is looking to advance its thought leadership on affordable healthcare, for instance, look out for potential changes in federal health insurance policies or announcements about premium increases and use these as opportunities to promote your ideas and opinions. Don't just wait for the phone to ring, make sure you're actively promoting your work and ideas to reporters.

PART 5

A. is Appealing

CHAPTER 15

Powerful Press Releases

While we discussed press releases a bit in the toolkit section, we think it's important to dig deeper and talk about how to make sure your press releases are hitting the mark with modern reporters and editors. When reporting teams were larger and news holes were bigger, you could usually count on at least some of your releases hitting pay dirt. Today, that press release may never even get opened. That's especially true if you don't take the time to make it stand out.

When your nonprofit sends a press release to a reporter or editor, it's immediately facing stiff competition for coverage. Journalists can receive hundreds of releases each week, and depending on what those reporters cover and who they work for, they only have time to report a handful of stories.

With that in mind, here are a few ways to stand out from the crowd and provide the media with something useful:

Avoid flat headlines. Instead of providing headlines that repeat the basic facts in the release, strive to create headlines that put the release in context. Many news releases include headlines that mimic the first sentence of the release rather than provide a colorful hook that shows why the release offers them something unique and different.

Include a well-considered quote. This can be a great tool. It can help you convince the journalist that your announcement is newsworthy. It also gives you the chance to write part of the story. Journalists know that strong quotes make their job easier by ensuring that they'll have a quote to include in the story even if they don't gather something useful from their interviews. But the sad truth is that the quote is considered a throwaway in many releases.

Elements of a Good Quote

Amplify, don't rehash. A good quote should add context and color to your announcement. It shouldn't merely repeat what you're announcing or say something obvious. For example, if you're announcing the hiring of a new executive director, try to avoid using an obvious quote from your board chair about how great the hire is. Make it something that tells the reader why this new hire is a good choice and what the person will bring to the organization.

A poor example: "The Sunshine Hospital Board of Directors is pleased to announce the hiring of Jane Smith as our new executive director. She is a great choice, and we'd like to congratulate her on the appointment."

A good example: "When we interviewed Jane, it was clear that she brings the passion, energy, and expertise that we need to lead Sunshine's upcoming expansion. She knows the needs of our patients and has a great understanding of how to properly manage capital projects."

Always attribute appropriately. A good quote always should be accompanied by the name and title of the person who is speaking. As a rule, news accounts use "said" or "says." Avoid "exclaimed," "remarked," "stated," or similar terms.

Avoid fragments. Ideally, the quote should be at least one full sentence.

Interview the speaker. Most news releases include at least one quote from an official with the organization that is issuing the release. Many communications pros make the mistake of ghost-writing carefully crafted quotes for their organizations' executive directors or CEOs and plunking them into the middle of their releases. If this is your current MO, we implore you to try a different approach with your next release.

Instead, schedule a 10- to 15-minute interview with the person you wish to quote. This will ensure that you're getting the person's own words, and it will likely provide you with insights that will help you frame the rest of the release. In your interview, ask the person why this announcement is important, what it will mean for your organization, and what it will mean for the people or community your organization serves. Also, take careful notes and be on the lookout for colorful phrases and anecdotes that can form the basis of your quote.

Sprinkle, don't pour. You should aim to include one or two strong quotes in the body of your releases. Remember: quotes are there to amplify and add context and color.

Get permission. Because you're writing the release on behalf of your organization, you do have some license to massage your quotes to make them more colorful or powerful. But you should make sure they capture the true meaning that your subject was trying to convey. Once you've written the quote, give the original source an opportunity to review it for accuracy.

Lay off the jargon. While it might seem smart to include buzzwords and insider language, good reporters will often have a visceral reaction to jargon-laden quotes. If you're looking for the most positive reaction, use clear, concise, and powerful language, language that came straight from the mouth of your expert in your interview. If you read the quote and it sounds like something that was carefully written rather than something that was actually said, it's probably not going to hit the mark.

Standing Out In a Sea Of Mediocrity

Your nonprofit faces long odds whenever it sends a press release. The good news is that you have an opportunity to stand out in this sea of mediocrity. You simply need to invest enough time to make sure your release provides reporters with the context and color they want.

Even under the best of circumstances, your release is competing with dozens of other releases and story ideas to earn that journalist's attention. And even if that journalist opens and reads your announcement, you must still sell the idea that yours is a story worth covering.

Using Visuals: Photos, Videos and Graphics

As people who earn a living largely through the written word, it's difficult for us to admit that when we're pitching a story to the media, words aren't enough.

Remember that today's reporters are being asked to do more than just write stories. Often, they are shooting photos and video, developing graphics and recording audio to accompany their written pieces. As a result, it shouldn't surprise anyone who works in nonprofit communications that strong photos and videos are essential to getting attention.

But when nonprofits reach out to the media, it's amazing how many of them rely solely on written materials to pitch their stories.

While a well-written press release with a grabby headline and a juicy news hook might have been enough to get reporters to pick up the phone a decade ago, that's usually not the case anymore. In today's environment, when competition for media attention is fiercer than ever, and many media organizations are looking for ready-made content, you need more.

Your written message will have a better chance of connecting if it is amplified with visuals. Otherwise, all of the time you spend crafting that release is likely to be wasted.

But don't just take our word for it.

News releases that are accompanied by a single visual asset—a photo, logo, or infographic—are 92 percent more likely to be seen online than a simple text release, according to an analysis by PR Newswire, which distributes content to the media on behalf of companies and nonprofits. And the more visuals you have, the better those numbers become. Those that include multiple media elements outpace text releases by more than 5.5 times.

Despite those numbers, though, PR Newswire found that 86 percent of the news releases published on its platform don't include visual elements.

Those numbers point to a great opportunity. By simply adding some smart visual elements to your next release, you will dramatically increase your odds of having your release seen. And not only will you be seen, you will have a leg up on getting your news picked up by the media. You also have a greater chance of getting your photo or graphic published in the newspaper or on a website.

This isn't only true if you're trying to get placement on a new media website like Buzzfeed or Upworthy. Peter's previous employer, *The Chronicle of Philanthropy*, didn't have a staff photographer. A little-known secret in the nonprofit world was that *The Chronicle* relies heavily on submitted photos, and nonprofits that have compelling photography of their work and programs have a stronger chance of getting into its pages than those that don't.

The challenge, of course, is that compelling visuals don't merely fall out of the sky. That's why 86 percent of those PR Newswire releases are text only.

But there are a few things nonprofits can do to incorporate strong photos, graphics, and videos into their media-relations efforts.

Take a step back. It sounds simple, but it's important to think about visuals whenever you plan an announcement, campaign, or event. And you need to start that thinking at the very beginning of the process.

If you're producing a new report, are there graphics you can generate to help show the key findings? If you're planning a new campaign, are there photos or videos that you can use or develop to help tell your story? It's important to plan for these elements early, rather than waiting until the end of the process.

Show your work. Your nonprofit's work is interesting. Instead of taking grip-and-grin or "happy snaps" of people posing at your fundraising dinner or donors presenting your executive director with a big check, find a talented volunteer who might be willing to take pictures of your team in action, or of beneficiaries of your organization's work.

If you have data that shows your impact or demonstrates the need for your programs, take time to develop simple graphics that help tell those stories.

In time, you should be able to build a library or "bank" of interesting images that you can use in conjunction with your pitches and releases.

Use what's free. While we strongly recommend investing in photography and videography (or finding talented volunteers or supporters to chronicle your work), there are also a number of no-cost ways to find compelling photos.

The photo-sharing site Flickr has a rich library of photos licensed under Creative Commons, many of which you can use for nothing more than attribution. New photo resources seem to be coming online every day.

Explore graphics. For nonprofits that are looking to create graphics on a budget, there are a number of free online tools that will help you build clean, easy-to-read charts and tables. Some of our favorites include Canva (which makes graphic design simple), and Piktochart (which is great for infographics).

Attracting Coverage for Data and Reports

Data and research can be powerful tools for nonprofits looking to call attention to their work. This is especially true if your organization is looking for media coverage. It bears repeating that reporters and editors love to latch on to stories that are based on new research or reveal an emerging trend.

If your nonprofit conducts an annual survey, collects data about the impact of its work, or has seen significant growth in fundraising or volunteering, chances are you have a great story to pitch to the news media.

Most nonprofits (and businesses, too) have a difficult time pitching stories about their data and research.

And it's easy to see why.

When you're confronted with spreadsheets full of numbers, it's not always simple to spot the story that's buried in all of those rows and columns.

So how do you find stories in your data?

It all starts with asking the right questions. In the same way a reporter interviews a source or a detective interviews a witness, you need to interview your data; ask questions that will help draw the conclusions you need to go forward.

If you ask the right questions, you'll likely find stories in your data that you can ultimately pitch to the media. You'll also likely gain insights that will help your organization better understand its work and impact.

Here are some questions you can try to ask when you're "interviewing" your data or research:

What has changed?

It might seem obvious, but if you have data that spans a period of time, the first thing you should try to explore is what has changed during that time.

Was there an increase in the number of people coming into your hospital's emergency room? Was there a decline in the amount of federal money that supports a key program? Has your organization been able to serve more people or raise more money?

If you can find interesting changes over time, you're on your way to finding a story to tell.

Usually, the next step after you find the trend is to determine why it's happening. Once you've found that trend, talk to key people inside your organization who can explain what is driving the trend.

If you can develop a pitch that spotlights a trend and offers the theory behind it, you're serving a story on a silver platter to a smart reporter.

What are the outliers?

When you're examining data, some of the best stories can be found in the outliers—the data outside the norm.

It's important when you're looking at your data or research that you isolate those outliers and find out why they happened and what they mean for the larger dataset.

Peter works with the Peer-to-Peer Professional (P2P) Forum to analyze and produce its annual report on the nation's 30 largest peer-to-peer fundraising programs. As part of that work he's looking for story angles that the organization can pitch to reporters.

Some years, that task is more difficult than others.

For example, when we compared the total raised by those top 30 programs year over year, the figure was essentially flat. It's not much of a story to say that nothing changed.

But when we isolated the outliers—the programs with fundraising decreases that were much larger than the norm—we noticed an intriguing trend. If we excluded two large and well-established charities that experienced the biggest declines, fundraising totals actually increased by a healthy amount for everyone else.

We had our story.

The largest, most established programs were struggling while a number of smaller, younger programs were growing quickly.

It was a meaty storyline that revealed a newsworthy trend. It was so newsworthy, in fact, that it landed coverage from NPR's Morning Edition, which did a feature story on a new wave of peer-to-peer fundraising programs based off of the data.

How can we group information?

You can also find great stories in your data by figuring out how you can group information within your dataset.

In the P2P Forum example, we were able to group information by type of campaign—big, established programs versus smaller, newer programs.

You might be able to group your organization's programs in other ways: by the age or race of those receiving services, by the home neighborhoods of your supporters, or by the income or political ideology of people who support a key piece of legislation your organization supports.

Sort your information in different ways to see if you can find patterns among these groups. As patterns emerge, explore why they're happening and whether they reveal an important insight.

What is surprising?

Most people love a story with an unexpected twist. If your data reveals something that surprises you or challenges what you think you know, chances are it will do the same when you pitch it to a reporter or editor.

If you ask these questions about your data, you're likely to find something that's newsworthy.

But you still need to attract the attention of the reporter or editor who will ultimately decide whether to write a story or air a report about your findings.

That leads us to a bonus question:

How do we pitch our data story?

There's no one answer because each story is different. But you should always try to follow one key principle: keep it simple.

Think about the key story you want to tell, and focus your pitch on how the data explains that story.

Matt Scharpnick, cofounder of Elefint Designs, which specializes in data visualization work for nonprofits, says that the key to a great data visualization is to focus on one or two key pieces of data that tell your story. The same should be true when you're pitching a story about data to a reporter. Focus on one or two key findings and make those the focus of your pitch. Resist the urge to throw tons of statistics into your introductory email or release.

"For me, it all starts with the story," Scharpnick says. "I ask myself, 'What is the most important thing people need to understand?' I often consider what people misunderstand or are intimidated by, where they tune out or give up. Then the job of the visualization becomes to show at least this one thing clearly."

You also should offer to provide the full report or data set to the reporter so the reporter can see your work and explore storylines.

But if you've interviewed your data correctly, chances are the story you pitch will become the story the reporter chooses to tell.

When Is It Time To Outsource Your Media Relations?

O ur mission with this book is to create a resource that will help even the smallest nonprofit create and execute a successful media relations strategy. We've used the strategies and tactics outlined throughout this book with nonprofits and foundations of all sizes—and we've gotten results. We know that you can, too, even if you have only a few hours a week to invest in your organization's media relations efforts.

Are Your In-house Resources Enough?

But there are times when your in-house resources simply aren't enough. And there are also times when you might need outside help to ensure your organization is able to take advantage of an important media opportunity or navigate a crisis. In these cases, your organization will likely consider working with an outside firm.

When does it make sense to consider outsourcing your media relations work? Here are a few situations when it might make sense:

- Your board has approved an ambitious new strategic plan for your organization—one that will require extensive outreach to your supporters and your community. An outside firm can use its experience in media relations to help you identify key messages and execute a campaign that will help explain your new plan to your target audiences.

- Your organization has been suddenly thrown into the center of a controversy and you don't have enough in-house support to develop a communications strategy for handling the crisis—and for handling the media inquiries that accompany it.

- You are looking to help your executive director develop their voice as a thought leader, but they don't have much experience writing opinion pieces, delivering speeches, or appearing before the camera. An outside firm can work with them—and you—to identify opportunities, develop ghostwritten pieces, or provide media and speech training services.

- Your nonprofit is looking to generate media attention outside of its local market and decides that it needs the support of an outside firm that already has the contacts and credibility to help your organization get noticed by out-of-town or national media members.

In each of the cases above—and in many others—an outside agency or specialist can help your organization achieve results that would be a stretch with your existing resources. If you do your homework, you can often find experts who specialize in the type of media work you need (such as crisis communications, media training, or ghostwriting). And some firms specialize in working with nonprofits and foundations.

How do you find the right expert or firm? It helps to answer a few key questions up front:

- **What are we looking to achieve?** It always helps to know your goals before you start shopping for a consultant or firm. This will help you identify what you're looking for, and search for companies and people who specialize in meeting your needs. If you're looking for help with a national campaign, for example, a local firm might not be the best fit. If you're looking to develop your presence with a specific audience, you might search for companies that have experience with media outlets that hit that audience.

- **What is your timeline?** Are you looking for something short term? Or ongoing help? Having an idea of your needs will help you provide potential consultants with the parameters they need to bid on your project.

- **What is your budget?** Before you start searching for help, have a sense of how much money you are willing to invest in the effort. Many consultants can design a scope of work for you that fits your budget.

Outsourcing media relations can get expensive. But it doesn't have to. There are various levels of outsourcing including:

- **Full-service firms.** Full-service marketing and PR firms often have a wide range of capabilities. For instance, they can not only design your strategy, but they can also train staff, write press releases, and conduct media outreach on your behalf. If your needs are extensive, a full-service firm might be your best bet. But there are often drawbacks. Some larger firms put their less experienced staff members on projects for nonprofits or take a more cookie-cutter approach to their work. If you're looking at a full-service firm, we recommend taking the time to find out who will actually be working with your organization and whether they have experience working with nonprofits and connecting with reporters who cover your areas of interest.

- **Specialty firms**. If your organization already has some internal resources for its media relations or has a specific need or project, a speciality firm might be your best bet. A specialty firm might not have the range of capabilities of a full-service company, but if your needs are more specific or short term, it can often give you exactly what you need. Peter's firm, for instance, specializes in getting foundations and nonprofits mentions in print media and radio. Other companies are better at earning spots on national television.

- **Freelancers**: If your budget is smaller, or if you simply need an extra set of hands to carry out your strategy, you can hire a freelancer. Freelancers often need more direction and specific assignments. But they are also often able to provide you with what you need, quickly.

Before hiring an outside firm or freelancer, Mary Jamis—president of M Creative, a North Carolina consultancy that works with nonprofits, universities, and foundations—recommends nonprofits take time to assess whether the contractor is a good cultural fit. She also recommends that they pay attention to how the firm talks about its work.

"Ask the firm to share a relevant case study or two," Jamis says. "Are there compelling insights or stories that led them to equally compelling creative solutions?

Ultimately, you want to make sure that you hire an agency or a person that can quickly understand who you are and what you want to accomplish—and that has the technical skills and contacts to deliver results

PART 6

T. is Targeted

CHAPTER 16

Identifying and Cultivating Media Outlets

When you open your email box, which messages are you most likely to open: generic emails from an unknown person or personal notes sent by someone you know?

The answer to this question is obvious, right? You're going to open the personal message first.

And you're more likely to trust that message than you would a message that comes from a stranger.

As you think about your media-relations strategy, it's important to think about it in terms of how you can become a trusted source to reporters and editors. Ultimately, you want to develop a reputation where, whenever a journalist sees your name in their inbox, they feel compelled to open your note, read it, and reply.

If you are just another unrecognizable name, you're less likely to get their attention.

Journalists, after all, are people. Busy people who receive TONS of emails.

As a result, it is important to make sure you're doing much more than spamming them with generic pitches. You want to instead give them valuable material—and build a level of trust that helps you stand out from the crowd.

How do you develop this reputation? One effective approach is to think about your media relationships strategically. It's difficult to do this if you cast a wide net. You're better served by identifying a handful of high-value journalists and begin courting them with personal outreach that speaks to the beats they cover.

You can begin to identify those high-value relationships by referring back to the answers identified in Setting Goals from Chapter Six:

- What are your organization's goals?
- Which audiences or people do you need to connect with to reach those goals?
- Which media outlets are most likely to reach those audiences?

Once you've identified those outlets, you can then determine which reporters and editors work at those outlets and begin the process of building relationships with those journalists.

Developing Relationships

The best fundraisers at your nonprofit aren't successful because they are great talkers. They are successful because they are great listeners.

They spend a lot of time learning about their donors' motivations—finding out what they want to accomplish with their money and what type of impact they want to make on the world. They learn about their donors' values, their families, and their careers. And they also make it clear that they are there to support the donor.

It's only after they truly understand the donor that the most successful fundraisers make their asks. And because they have taken the time to build trust and gather information, they are able to make bigger and better asks—and close larger and more substantial gifts.

No, we didn't just pull a switcheroo and turn this into a book about fundraising. We're still talking about media relations but we raise this analogy because the relationships you forge with local newspaper reporters, TV news desk editors, and radio producers are built on the same principles as the relationships that are built in your organization's development office.

And, as with all good relationships, productive relationships with journalists are built not by forcing what you want on the other person, but rather on finding out how you can help serve the needs of the other person. This begins with listening—not pitching.

Yes, you are ultimately building these relationships because you want to get positive coverage for your organization. But it's important to understand what the journalist needs, the pressures they face, and how you can help fill those needs.

"Being a good partner isn't just about telling my story," says Tara Collins, former newspaper reporter turned nonprofit communications director with Rup Co. "It's about relating data and being a thought leader, door opener, and to be generous with contact, resource and story ideas. You have to treat journalists like any other relationship with a professional colleague. Their respect for you will be reflected in their writing."

Doing this effectively means discovering how they work and creating opportunities to build rapport. Below are some suggestions on how to build these important relationships:

Respect their time. Learn about their deadlines and make sure you are cognizant of when is not a good time to reach out. Respect those deadlines, as well, when you're helping them with a story. Make sure you provide information or photos well in advance. Newspapers, radio shows, and television news programs have daily deadlines while magazines and trade publications plan ahead. To avoid missing an opportunity, you should ask about special features like event previews or sector reports where the journalists will be actively looking for contributions from organizations like yours.

Help them do their jobs. Journalists rely on people like you for story ideas, data, tips, and access to interviews—and they are often working under tight deadlines. One of the best ways to establish productive relations is to help reporters accomplish their own objectives by providing them with information and other sources, respecting deadlines, and anticipating questions so that you are prepared to answer on the spot.

Learn their preferences. Find out what their requirements are because most journalists are incredibly busy. Ask them when it would be a good time to call back, offer to take them for coffee, or arrange to meet them at an event.

You can also create opportunities for them to meet with new sources and gain new perspectives that can help them with future reporting. Collins says her organization has found tremendous success arranging press luncheons. She invites members of the media to her organization for meetings about important issues on their beats.

"I find that more press people come to our event when I have food," Collins says. "We did a press conference for a solar installation and invited eight reporters. I invited them to just come lunch on me and you don't have to cover the story. It gave them an opportunity to network and meet new people that could provide resources."

Stay in touch. Many media relations professionals make the mistake of only reaching out to reporters when they are making a story pitch or sending a formal news release. But the most successful media relations pros make a point of reaching out regularly—even when they aren't making an ask. You can keep in touch through phone calls, emails, and social media correspondence—though we should note that most reporters prefer emails over calls. It can be as simple as complimenting them on a story you enjoyed or asking what they are working on. You don't need to pester. But if you can make it clear that you're accessible and that you have something meaningful to share, it will go a long way when they're looking for a source or when you have something that you're hoping to pitch.

Know what they need. The fastest way to turn off a reporter is to pepper them with pitches that they don't want. If you're cultivating a relationship with an investigative reporter, avoid sending pitches for human-interest stories.

It is also worth cultivating relationships with the freelance journalists who write for the publications that you are targeting. They are often looking for quotes, information, and ideas. If you help them, they will come back to you for your input.

Below are some tips for being a useful resource for journalists:
- Establish a friendship on social media.
- Acknowledge their work (If you notice a great story posted by a journalist in your community, let them know).

137

- Position your spokespeople as sources and thought leaders.
- Develop a specific process to get them to take your calls and meet with you in person.
- Become a valued resource, and go above and beyond the usual expectations. Be willing to feed reporters reliable sources—even ones that don't involve your nonprofit. Take the time to connect a reporter to a good story or source— even if it's not someone from your organization. It's another relationship-building tool, and the source you offer is likely to speak positively about you to the reporter.

Cultivating Your Database

As you identify the reporters and editors you'd like to cultivate, it's important to build a media list that documents the key contacts that would be interested in stories about your business or area of expertise. These media contacts should include journalists, reporters, bloggers, producers, freelance writers, and editors. Some nonprofits choose to hire PR companies to build or provide this type of database.

Of course, your media list will include the names and contact info of reporters and editors. But it can also include much more.

Some nonprofits build robust databases that include information about the topics these reporters cover, the type of outlet they work for (print, online, radio, podcast, etc.), and the readership or audience size. You can also include information about the editorial calendar and the deadlines of the media you're targeting. This will give your story the best chance of getting published. It is also helpful to include social media contact information—such as Twitter handles.

Update your list regularly because your media contacts will often change roles or beats. One way to keep track of this info is to read industry newsletters and blogs such as Fishbowl, Min, and MediaBistro. Staying on top of changes within media outlets will ensure that your media list stays up to date.

Finding Media Contacts

Research is key when building your media lists.

You can use programs like Cision, FinderBinder, and Google to search for lists; however, sometimes these data are not up to date or are costly to access. As a result, you'll likely need to do a lot of your own digging by visiting the websites of your priority outlets and searching for the bylines of reporters who cover stories that relate to your organization. You should also try to identify key editors and find information about how to submit opinion pieces and letters to the editor.

Some outlets will list staff email addresses and phone numbers. Others make it a bit more difficult to track. In these cases, you might have to resort to the old-fashioned tactic of calling the newsroom to discover the contact info for the journalists you most want to reach. It's important to pay attention to job title and beat. After all, you probably don't want to send your fundraising gala pitch to the crime reporter.

Identifying Reporters Speaking To Your Key Audience

We have already covered some of the basics of identifying your target audience but just to recap, the first thing you need to decide when creating your media list is who your target audiences are and how to best reach them. Start by researching what your target audiences are interested in and how they prefer to consume information, including blogs, websites, TV programs, newspapers, or magazines. Discovering how your target audience chooses to consume information has become easier with social media data.

Look at articles written about your topic in your target publications and note the journalists who wrote these stories. Try using Google Alerts for related topics to track who is covering similar stories. You might also consider liking and sharing the journalist's stories on social media. If you can help reporters get attention on Twitter or Facebook, you might also make it more likely that they'll connect with you, and follow your organization's work.

The Reward

Building relationships with journalists might not seem like a high priority in your communications strategy, but investing time and resources in building these relationships will pay off later. Finding that connection will not only improve the quality of coverage, but it can be of great benefit if your nonprofit ever needs to do quick damage control. It sounds obvious that journalists are human, but remember that their leanings are often reflected in their work. If they cover nonprofits, they probably care about their causes.

CHAPTER 17

Pitching to the Nonprofit Trade Press

When nonprofits build their media relations strategies, they often focus on getting their stories told in the local media or in the national mainstream press.

But they often overlook an important potential avenue for spreading the word about their work—the trade press.

Trade publications cover specific industries and often have very specialized audiences. If your nonprofit has a mission in health-care, education, or the environment, you're likely already aware of the trade publications and websites that are specific to those missions.

Working with a trade outlet requires a somewhat different approach than working with a local newspaper or television station.

To illustrate how this works, let's consider how to pitch to the trade media in an industry that we're all familiar with—the trades that cover nonprofits and foundations.

These publications and websites—which include *The Chronicle of Philanthropy, Inside Philanthropy, Nonprofit Quarterly, The*

Nonprofit Times, Stanford Social Innovation Review, and many others—can be incredibly valuable to nonprofits.

This is especially true for nonprofits that are looking to earn the attention of potential funders or brand their organizations as experts in fundraising, nonprofit management, talent management, or storytelling.

Before you start sending these outlets the same pitches you make to the general media, keep in mind that stories that are covered by these outlets are different than those that are covered by a mainstream outlet. After all, The Chronicle of Philanthropy does not have the same focus as The Houston Chronicle.

That's because the audience is very different to what you'll find in a mainstream publication. These outlets cater to providing people inside the nonprofit and foundation world with information that can help them be more effective in their work. As a result, they are focused on finding stories that speak to a trend that is happening in the industry, a best practice that others can learn from, or something that challenges the status quo.

The Chronicle of Philanthropy and *The Nonprofit Times* are less interested in the fact that you've launched a new fundraising campaign than they are in learning about how you're conducting the campaign. Have you embraced a different tactic? Are you using social media or mobile technology in a new way? Are you appealing to a specific type of donor and, if so, how?

If you're serious about getting your organization featured in one of these outlets, you need to think differently about how you structure your pitches.

Rather than thinking about what the public would find

interesting about your work, you need to instead think about your pitch in terms of what a peer who works at a nonprofit would find interesting.

If you were talking to a nonprofit executive director or development director at a cocktail party, what would they be interested in knowing about what's really happening at your organization?

If you can answer that question, chances are you have a good chance at offering an idea or angle that would appeal to one of the industry's trade outlets.

But you shouldn't stop there. Here are some other steps you can take to get on their radar:

Get to Know Them

The cardinal rule of effective media relations is to know the outlets and reporters you're trying to pitch. Take the time to read, watch, and listen to their content and develop an understanding of what they cover and how they cover it. You'll start to see patterns in the types of stories that they like to pursue and who they quote.

As you gain that understanding, you'll start to see how your nonprofit fits in with their coverage.

Being a regular reader also provides you with an opening for reaching out. If a story really resonated with you—or if you think they missed a key point in their coverage of an important issue—this offers you an opportunity to reach out to the reporter and let them know your thoughts.

By doing so, you'll likely start a conversation that could lead to that reporter reaching out to you for comment the next time they cover that issue.

Identify Trends

The trade press is always interested in identifying trends in how nonprofits are doing their work, the types of projects getting support from funders, and how the economy and legislation are affecting the nonprofit world.

Often, your organization is uniquely qualified to offer insights on these trends because you're living them.

While you might think it's inside baseball that your school's development team is now holding text-a-thons instead of phone-a-thons to connect with young alumni, the trades thrive on inside baseball.

It's what they cover and what their audience expects.

Think about how your organization is either shaping, or being shaped by, a trend and share that information with a trade reporter. It could lead to your executive director being called as a source or your nonprofit being spotlighted as an example.

Identify What's Unique

During Peter's time at *The Chronicle of Philanthropy,* he received thousands of releases from organizations about annual dinners, fundraising events, and award recipients. Rarely did those releases actually identify what would make their event or award interesting to other nonprofit professionals.

If you're going to take the time to send a release to a trade publication, invest a little bit of extra time to customize it. Otherwise, you are guaranteeing that that release will end up in the trash.

For example, think about what makes your annual dinner unique. During the early days of social media, Peter wrote a piece about a small nonprofit that set up a Twitter table at a fundraising luncheon so that its supporters could share what was happening on social media and ask for donations from folks who weren't at the lunch.

If you can identify how your organization is taking a different approach or achieving unusual results, you have something to share with the trades—regardless of the industry they cover.

If you can't, then you're better off not sending the release. and waiting until you have something useful.

Look at Your Data

For reporters who cover nonprofits, good data is often hard to find.

If your organization has numbers that show growth in specific forms of fundraising, can shed light on trends in benefits costs, or can offer insights into which fundraising channels are most effective, you are likely to get the attention of the nonprofit trade press.

Be constantly on the lookout for items in your data that are noteworthy and, when possible, get permission to share it.

Find an Interesting Personality

Like most media, the nonprofit trade press isn't just looking for hard news, trends, and data.

It also likes to profile interesting people who work in the field. But they often struggle to find profile subjects who are outside of the "usual suspects" who dominate their pages.

Be on the lookout for people within your organization who are taking an interesting approach to their work or who might be willing to open their doors to a reporter to show them what it's like to walk in their shoes.

There's an adage in the media that everybody has a story—and it's an adage because it's true. Your nonprofit is likely full of people who have compelling stories to tell about why they do what they do—and how they do it.

When you find those stories, don't be afraid to share them with the trades.

Think About Visuals

As with mainstream media, photos and graphics offer another avenue for getting your organization into the nonprofit trade press.

Many of these outlets have big needs for photos and graphics to illustrate their stories—and unlike larger media outlets, small budgets for taking photos and acquiring images.

If your organization has a strong library of photos that showcase its work or has developed infographics and other materials that speak to interesting trends, it would be worth your while to reach out to the editors of these publications and let them know that you have images to share.

These images could end up illustrating an upcoming story—and they might open a door for a reporter to reach out and find out more about the story behind the photo.

Be Accessible

Like other types of media, reporters and editors for the nonprofit trades are often looking for reliable sources that they can reach out to when they have a tight deadline or are struggling to find the right perspective for a story.

As you study these outlets, find out who the reporters are that cover the issues that connect with your work, and let them know who you are and how your organization can help them.

In addition, make sure your website has a page for the media that makes it easy for reporters to find the right contact and to access previous announcements and releases.

The nonprofit trade press can be a great place for your organization to tell its story and gain visibility.

But to be successful, you need to take a different approach. By taking some extra time to think about your work through a different lens, your organization can get coverage through these outlets—no matter your size or mission.

Keep in mind, too, that these same rules also apply to other types of specialty media. If you're targeting outlets that have a niche audience around specific topics like the environment or health care, you will have much more success if you tailor your pitches to that particular niche—rather than trying to target them with angles that appeal to a more general audience.

Conclusion & Key Advice

Let's imagine that you were recently hired to serve as the one-person communications team for a small, locally-based nonprofit that is working to ensure that people living in a neighborhood with economic challenges have access to affordable, healthy food.

Needless to say, your budget for media relations is small—and your time is limited. But you recognize that you have an opportunity to change minds and raise additional support if you can get your story told in the media. And your executive director and the board of directors want to see some headlines.

In speaking with your predecessor, you learn that your new organization has tried_quite unsuccessfully_to get media attention for its fundraising events and for major announcements. But you also learn that these previous efforts were clearly the result of the spray-and-pray tactics that are common among small organizations. The nonprofit was essentially sending out bland releases to every outlet it could find, often at the last minute. Most of those releases were never read—and only rarely did your organization appear in a news story.

But you step into your new role with confidence knowing that you already have a blueprint—the G.R.E.A.T. model—for getting your organization's story told:

Goal Oriented. During your first weeks on the job, you meet with the executive director, the board chair, and other key staff members to understand your organization's biggest goals. You learn that the nonprofit is working to persuade the City Council to provide a tax incentive program to encourage a grocery store to invest in developing in the neighborhood and that it's devoting considerable attention to a new program that helps teach families how to cook healthy meals. In turn, your goal for your media relations efforts moves away from simply trying to get reporters to come and cover fundraising events, and instead focuses on broadening public support for the tax incentives and sharing stories about your healthy cooking program.

Responsive. You develop a set of key messages that are pre-written and easily accessible so that you have them at the ready when opportunities for coverage arise. You designate your executive director as a spokesperson for the organization and spend two hours per month getting her prepared on being a thought leader on your key issues. You create a simple 'Newsroom' page on your organization's website that provides key background about your work, downloadable images, recent press releases, and your contact info. When reporters call or email you looking for information or sources, you respond quickly and with relevant information.

Engaged. You review your goals and identify a handful of local reporters in your city who are most likely to cover stories about city government, health, and social issues. Instead of hitting them regularly with press releases that don't connect with their beats, you invest your time building relationships with them. You learn about what they cover and how they like to be pitched and make them aware that your organization has experts who can serve as knowledgeable sources for their reporting. You identify story ideas that fall on their beats and connect with your goals. You follow and engage with these reporters on social media.

Appealing. You develop a new template for your news releases—and make sure that they are always succinct and free from jargon. You are thoughtful about your pitches—ensuring that they include colorful hooks and connect to what the reporters cover.

Targeted. Knowing that your—and their—time is precious, you only approach your highest-value reporters when you are confident that you can provide them with something useful and when it helps advance your organization's goals. You commit to attempting to place two op-eds in the local newspaper during the course of your first year. You avoid sending blanket announcements about non-newsworthy items such as fundraising events without first finding a hook or idea that will appeal to your highest-value outlets.

As a result of this new approach, your organization starts to see results—even though it is devoting roughly the same amount of time to media relations that it did with its previous approach.

Not only are you showing up more regularly in the local media, you've started getting calls from reporters at national media outlets who, when researching the effort to bring healthy food to disadvantaged neighborhoods, found an op-ed that was written by your executive director online.

Better yet, these placements aren't just getting your organization's name in the paper, they're advancing your goals, connecting with your most valuable audiences.

Quite simply, the results have been G.R.E.A.T.

And Finally ...

As you begin to incorporate the G.R.E.A.T. model into your organization's media relations efforts, you'll likely need some extra advice and examples along the way to help guide your work. While we hope this book gives you the framework you need to be successful, we know you might need some inspiration along the way.

With that in mind, we've created an online appendix (which you can find at turn-two.co/ModernMedia) that will provide you with examples of successful press releases and op-eds—as well as other resources such as audience personas.

We also want to collect and share your success stories. If the advice from this book helps your organization land an important placement or navigate a challenge, we'd love to hear about it. You can share your story using a special form that appears with the online appendix or email Peter: peter@turn-two.co

We know you're going to have some great stories to share!

Appendix

For an online appendix visit turn-two.co/ModernMedia to get access to:

1. Sample Press Releases
2. Sample Personas
3. Updated Guides/Links to Modern Media Presentations

References By Chapter

Chapter One

Doctor, Ken. 2015. *Newsonomics: The halving of America's daily newsroom.* American Society of News Editors.

Chadwick, Nicole. 2014. "Revolutionizing the Newsroom: How Online and Mobile Technologies Have Changed Broadcast Journalism," *Nicole Chadwick.*

Huffington Post Blog, March 2016. "Let's all commit acts of citizen journalism" Michel Nigro.

Chapter Two

Chad Bowman, personal interview with Peter Panepento, February 24, 2017.

Chapter Six

TEKGROUP Online Newsroom Survey, 2015.

Cindy Olnick, personal interview with Antionette Kerr, January 3, 2017.

Chapter Seven

Ebony Hillsman, personal interview with Antionette Kerr, February 13, 2017.

Chapter Eight

Lidya K Osadchey, personal interview with Antionette Kerr, December 9, 2017.

Lidya K Osadchey, email correspondence, December 20, 2017.

Chapter Eleven

Christina Adeleke, Esq., personal interview with Antionette Kerr, March 1, 2017.

Chapter Twelve

Nieman Reports, 2009.

Christina Adeleke, Esq., personal interview with Antionette Kerr, March, 1 2017.

Chapter Thirteen

Denise Brosseau, email correspondence, February 13, 2017.

Denise Brosseau, personal interview with Antionette Kerr, February 11, 2017.

Trista Harris, personal interview with Antionette Kerr, February 23, 2017.

Claire Meyerhoff, personal interview with Antionette Kerr, December 19, 2016.

Claire Meyerhoff, Nonprofit Marketing Guide Webinar "Marketing Makeover Magic," April 28, 2015.

Chapter Fourteen

Matt Scharpnick, personal interview with Peter Panepento, June, 2015.

Chapter Fifteen

Mary Jamis, personal interview with Antionette Kerr, August 28, 2017.

Mary Jamis, email correspondence, August 28, 2017.

Chapter Sixteen

Tara Collins, personal interview with Peter Panepento, January 4, 2017.

Made in the USA
Coppell, TX
29 August 2020